Reading The Cantos

Reading the Cantos

The Study of Meaning in Ezra Pound

BY

NOEL STOCK

PANTHEON BOOKS

A Division of Random House, NEW YORK

232238

First American Edition

© Copyright, 1966, by Noel Stock

All rights reserved under International and Pan-American Copyright Conventions. Published in New York by Pantheon Books, a division of Random House, Inc. and in London, England by Routledge & Kegan Paul Ltd.

Library of Congress Catalog Card Number: 67-15071

Manufactured in the United States of America

CONTENTS

v

PREFACE

OF THE FOLLOWING PAGES it may be said that the aim is simpler than the result. I have tried to show what Ezra Pound has actually written in the *Cantos*, insisting upon what he has written as the necessary original around which any reading must revolve. At the same time I suggest that the work is nothing like advertised. That too much has been read into it which is simply not there. Too much taken for granted, for which there is no warrant in the text and scarce any or none in Pound's other writings.

Even Hugh Kenner and Donald Davie have erred in these respects. Both have written elaborate, learned and often penetrating studies of various aspects of the *Cantos*: Professor Kenner with the brilliance that is his trademark; Professor Davie, in his book, *Ezra Pound, Poet as Sculptor* (Routledge & Kegan Paul, 1965), with an ease that is truly admirable. For their task they possess many notable qualifications, but they lack at least one which might be fairly thought to be indispensable, namely the ability to distinguish between what the *Cantos* actually say and what they might have said had Pound written a more comprehensible work. They supplement the deficiencies of the former with arguments from the latter, which is of their own imagination. With the result that they cannot come to grips with the special problems which the work presents to the reader who wants to read it as poetry. Even George Dekker, who in his *Sailing after Knowledge* (Routledge & Kegan Paul, 1963) is sometimes more critical, and in some ways more valuable, than the other two, is far too easygoing in his assumptions about the text, and, like Professors Kenner and Davie, far too apt to accept, even if only indirectly, Pound's own estimates of his achievement. Much as we admire their work, and have profited thereby, the gap between what they say about the *Cantos* and what the *Cantos* say is far too wide for us to be able to accept them as interpreters.

It is one thing to comment on the difficulties or obscurities of a classic the general import of which has for long been accepted as a basis for admiration and disagreement. Quite another to treat as a classic a work which nobody has yet shown any signs of understanding. Our present task is not then to discuss the obscurities of a text in the main already understood, but to work out what the text means.

As it is not in the nature of this book to deal with textual problems, of which in the *Cantos* there are many, I have for convenience used recent editions readily available: *The Cantos of Ezra Pound* (Faber & Faber, London, 1954), *Section: Rock-Drill* (Faber & Faber, 1957), and *Thrones* (Faber & Faber, 1960), all of which are collected in the one-volume *The Cantos of Ezra Pound* (Faber & Faber, 1964). In the United States the *Cantos* are published by New Directions Publishing Corporation, New York. Generally I have not gone over ground already covered in my *Poet in Exile: Ezra Pound* (Manchester, 1964), or inserted information available in *The Annotated Index to the Cantos of Ezra Pound* (California, 1959). The latter, while incomplete—it goes only to the end of the Pisan section—and containing errors and omissions, is nevertheless indispensable. The names and dates of all other publications that have seemed relevant are worked into the text. The student who wants to follow the course of Pound's work in greater detail, will find the way considerably lightened by Donald Gallup's *Bibliography of Ezra Pound* (Rupert Hart-Davis, London, 1963).

I would like to take this opportunity to thank Mrs Dorothy Pound for permission to quote from published works of Ezra Pound.

NOEL STOCK

I

INTRODUCTION

THE MOST OBVIOUS aspect of the *Cantos* is that they are composed of at least eight separate sections, the continuity and interdependence of which are by no means obvious. The thing to do then is to begin at the beginning. To examine each section in order, taking note of connexions as we come upon them, but not inventing where we fail to find them. Such links would provide a means for considering the parts as belonging to a single poem and a starting-point for enquiry into the deeper question of form. But until they are discovered any talk of 'construction' is a waste of time.

It is not necessary to find all, or perhaps even half, the relations between the parts of a long poem. Not immediately, at any rate. But we must uncover a reasonable skeleton or we cannot begin to think of it as a self-contained work. We may sense or feel the wholeness before actually arriving at it. This is another matter. But until we are able to see some, at least, of the relations between the parts, such as it is possible to hold in the mind for logical analysis and development, we cannot speak of the work as coherent. Not that we must of necessity submit the relationships to such treatment, only they must be of a kind open to it. Not wholly so, necessarily, but enough to be able to communicate with the ground of realism which is naturally present in the working of the human mind.

Nor does it mean that a long poem must be a logical construction following step by step some philosophical system borrowed or home-made. Works of art obey other laws as well.

I

But they do not, and cannot, if they are true works, obey other laws alone. They must have some link, no matter how fine or roundabout, with a logical world, otherwise the mind could not come to terms with them. The great works, fewer perhaps than the past century or so of extreme self-consciousness in the face of Art might lead us to suppose, cohere at every level, and the levels are related. Logical connexion is a minimum, not a maximum, barely enough by itself, but without which the other relationships tend to give way to non-poetic ambiguity or disappear completely.

A danger with the *Cantos*, about which so much has been written by its author and others even while it has actually been in the making, is that we may too easily adjust our reading to what we have heard about them rather than to what we see on the page. Since the work is a coherent whole, there must be a network of relations and connexions. And not finding any we may take their existence for granted or even for our peace of mind imagine or invent them. We owe something to the individual poet whose work we are reading. But also to the literature and language without which neither the words written nor the words read have any meaning. A careful reading of the text is the way to do justice to both the work and the setting in and by which it exists.

One of the first things we notice is that the *Cantos* contain a number of pieces which can be extracted and read as separate short poems or fragments. This in itself is not positive evidence of anything except possibly a common ground with all other long poems. What is surprising is the unusually large number of such passages: not just one or two in the first thirty cantos, but dozens of short poems in various styles already employed by Pound in his earlier work. The opening canto is not far removed from 'The Seafarer' of 1911. It is technically more proficient perhaps, in that it incorporates devices which he had not learnt when he wrote the earlier piece. And it is mature in tone in a way that the other is not. But I am not so sure that 'The Seafarer' is not the better poetry. It is simple and direct, yet full of rhythmic vitality and universal imagery. Exactly the right tone is maintained throughout, with the result that it is an excellent embodiment of something the poet had within himself seeking a form.

Canto 1, on the other hand, which is a translation into Anglo-Saxon style of a Renaissance Latin translation of the *Odyssey*, is marred in several respects. The most important for our purposes here is that the Anglo-Saxon vehicle is not fully competent to carry the Homeric content, leading to suggestions of strain in the tone and diction. This is particularly noticeable in the direct speech, which falls between two stools. It is too artificial, or not artificial enough. Whether some of the differences are because one is an individual poem and the other the first canto of 'a Poem of some Length', remains to be seen. Canto 1 certainly does not seem to be connected in any immediate or obvious way with canto 2, nor for that matter with anything in the first hundred pages, except some odd references to Odysseus. If there are real links they will come to light as our reading progresses and deepens. What cannot be denied at the outset is that canto 1, taking away the last few lines, looks like a separate Poundian poem.

Other instances are easy to find. The fifteen lines in canto 7 beginning 'We also made ghostly visits,' and several other short sections in the same canto, are not immediately and obviously connected with their surroundings, not to the extent that they gain additional force, or communicate more, by being considered in this light. Canto 13, on Confucius, is quite self-contained and can only be connected with the canto before, or the canto after, by an intellectual construction which may or may not be justified by the text. The 'Hell' cantos (nos. 14 and 15) and the escape from Hell into the region of the heroes (first part of canto 16), hold together as a separate section because of the narrative continuity, implied or actual, which is so often absent from surrounding pages. In canto 20 we have at least three separate sections: three and a quarter pages devoted, quite arbitrarily as far as I can see, to Provence, Niccolò d'Este and the jungle of 'renewals'; the Lotus-eaters and companions of Odysseus; and the procession from 'and the cars

3

slowly' to the end of the canto. All may be connected but it is certainly not easy to see how. In canto 23 there are two separate short pieces beginning 'And the rose grown while I slept' and 'Leaf over leaf', which are not fully rounded poems but independent, as far as we can see, of their surroundings. In canto 25, an independent piece beginning 'they built out over the arches'; in canto 27, another running from 'And Tovarisch lay in the wind' to 'Laid never stone upon stone'; and several more in cantos 28 and 30. Canto 27 opens with the quotation 'Formando di disio nuova persona' ('And fashions a new person from desire') from Cavalcanti's Ballate XII. Its meaning is clear in the Ballate but a puzzle in the canto. It needs to be linked, presumably, with other parts of the same canto, or perhaps with other cantos, but the poet does not indicate where or which, and the reader who makes the effort is confronted by a choice of not very thrilling possibilities of about equal value. We look at Pound's translation of the original poem in his *Sonnets and Ballate of Guido Cavalcanti* (1912) but are still none the wiser. It is a case where finding the source doesn't seem to help. The meaning depends—or so we are forced to reason—upon some connexion inside the *Cantos*. But what, we do not know. Our inability to find a thread, or anything at all, which will enable us to understand what the poet is doing, is no good ground at this stage for declining to entertain the poem seriously. It is difficult and unsatisfactory, but there is too much in it which is good, and too much which indicates that he knows what he is doing, for us to be satisfied with such a conclusion.

Few difficulties in the *Cantos* are those of other modern poetry. They are not, in Pound, difficulties of subject-matter, or even essentially of communication. The subject-matter is mostly simple and straightforward and could be communicated without undue strain if the poet saw his task in this light. But two things intervene: a personal quirk and a theory about poetry. Because of the quirk, signs of which appear quite early in his career, he takes it for granted that the rest of the world somehow shares his own knowledge of his own life and experiences. It does not occur to him that his own views of his own encounters, especially mere passing incidents in far-off times and places, are not available to the world unless he re-creates them. We cannot see what he saw in a certain unrecorded situation in Spain in 1906, unless he tells us about it. We cannot see what he saw in the eyes of a figure from a fresco in Siena unless he gives us some idea—holds out some very definite, universal and intelligible thing independent of the fresco, yet related to it, through which we may grasp the significance of what he is trying to communicate.

When Pound gives only a mere fragment of some incident which he has never, or barely, referred to in some other place, I do not think that he is simply being cantankerous. Often for him the fragment is not a fragment any more than a key phrase known among youths who have been at college together, or a signal between husband and wife, is fragmentary. The fragment tells a story—for those who know. It is Pound's peculiarity to think that because he knows something *therefore* we know it too. There are signs of this in the lapses into informal language in the early books. But it shows more clearly several years later in the article 'How I Began', written for a London public, in which he suddenly recalls, without adequate explanation, college football heroes of his own student days or earlier. We encounter it again in the first canto. After two pages of fairly straightforward narrative, during which Odysseus descends into the underworld and Tiresias delivers his soothsay, we are suddenly confronted with: 'Lie quiet Divus. I mean, that is Andreas Divus, In officina Wecheli, 1538, out of Homer.' We may suppose that most people guess immediately who this Divus is (the Latin translator through whom Pound has rendered Homer into 'Anglo-Saxon') because they have already heard about him from some commentator or read about him in the second part of Pound's 'Early Translators of Homer' first published in the *Egoist* of September 1918 and available later in *Make It New* (1934) and the *Literary Essays* (1954):

In the year of grace 1906, 1908, or 1910 I picked up from the Paris quais a Latin version of the *Odyssey* by Andreas

Divus Justinopolitanus (Parisiis, In officina Christiani Wecheli, MDXXXVIII), the volume containing also the *Batrachomyomachia*, by Aldus Manutius, and the *Hymni Deorum* rendered by Georgius Dartona Cretensis. I lost a Latin *Iliads* for the economy of four francs, these coins being at that time scarcer with me than they should be with any man of my tastes and abilities.

But I cannot help wondering how long it would take us to work it out unaided. Even the additional phrase, 'plucked from a Paris stall', which was included in an earlier cancelled version of canto 1, does not bridge the essential gap between Pound and his reader; does not tell us who Divus is, or why he is there. The importance of this digression is twofold. It may prevent us from looking for, and discovering, in many parts of the *Cantos* subtleties and profundities which do not exist. And secondly it may help us to concentrate on what is actually written there. Generally Pound describes things he has seen or heard. Any meaning is supposed to rise from the 'object', or 'objects' in relation. When we fail to understand a passage the reason often is that we cannot see what Pound is describing because he has given us too small a fragment. Too small for us to be able to make out the shape of the whole and the necessary background. Our failure does not mean that we have missed the meaning but that we are unable to see the 'objects' or something essential in the background which is supposed to give rise to the meaning. In other words the *Cantos* very often mean just what they say. If they fail to communicate we had best look, not for the hidden significance of what is on the page, but rather for the missing pieces, without which we cannot even see the primary 'object' through which the poet might indicate a deeper meaning. We must concentrate therefore on what is on the page. For this represents, even if it does not adequately describe, the all-important 'object'. A rule which applies equally to quotations as well. Pound transcribes a great deal from others and alludes also to his own work. The quotation—sometimes the merest fragment—represents the passage, the page, or the book from which it is taken. Or sometimes, I suspect, Pound's views on

6

the work rather than the work itself. This does not make for easy reading and even a fragment like 'Sed et universus' in canto 27 might puzzle indefinitely if we did not come upon, or remember, the 'Lingua Toscana' chapter in *The Spirit of Romance*.

Much of the trouble lies in the personal quirk. But the effect is complicated by his theory that in poetry you can deal with the 'poetic part' of your subject and leave the 'prose part' aside. This we must take into account when considering the 'method of the *Cantos*'. Ernest Fenollosa contributed his share especially with his essay on 'The Chinese Written Character', but that was later and as much a confirmation of Pound's ideas as an addition to his actual practice. The 'method' derives in large part from:

(1) The personal peculiarity.

(2) The early 'method' outlined in a letter to William Carlos Williams in 1908:

'To me the short so-called dramatic lyric—at any rate the sort of thing I do—is the poetic part of a drama the rest of which (to me the prose part) is left to the reader's imagination or implied or set in a short note. I catch the character I happen to be interested in at the moment he interests me. . . And the rest of the play would bore me and presumably the audience...'

(3) A technique of contrast, of 'beauty' versus 'squalor', which he approached in 1910 or 1911 in an unpublished long poem called 'Redondillas'. He later found it being put to mature use in Joyce, as noted in his review of *Portrait of the Artist as a Young Man* in the *Future* of May 1918: 'On almost every page of Joyce you will find just such swift alternation of subjective beauty and external shabbiness, squalor and sordidness. It is the bass and treble of his method.'

If the author's mind works in this way the poem is at once simpler and more difficult than we have allowed. Simpler, in that we are no longer likely to go hunting for hidden meanings and implications that do not exist. More difficult, in that there are gaps which may be permanent. If it be objected that this explanation is not dependent on the text, I can only say that the difficulties of the poem do in fact point in this direction, and that a growing acquaintance with the work as a whole yields evidence connecting the working of his mind with the strange ordering of the poem and the many blanks.

If we go back to the early poems we see that the sources of his obscurity are not in technique, not in an inability to say what he wanted to say. A young man with the skills of 'Famam Librosque Cano' and 'Threnos' already mastered by the time he was 23, who went on perfecting them, consistently, through *Ripostes, Lustra, Cathay* and *Mauberley*, was not likely to have had trouble later with communication in the ordinary sense, when what he had to convey in the *Cantos* were mostly 'objects', things, facts, conversations. Communication may not always be satisfactory when conducted in this way. And it is certain that some of the worst obscurities in the *Cantos* are due to this method, as we shall see later. But the distinction I wish to make is between method and the misuse of. It would be unfair to blame the method in cases where the fault lies in its use. It would be wrong to say that an 'object' fails to communicate when what we really mean, or should say, is that the 'object', or whatever it is Pound wants us to *see*, is not clearly drawn, or that we have been given only an unidentifiable fragment in its place. Perhaps the most serious signs of this weakness in the poetry before the *Cantos* are in *Mauberley*, which, for all its mastery, is affected by it. The first line of poem VI (*Yeux Glaques*), 'Gladstone was still respected', is not sharp enough for the irony it is supposed, apparently, to carry. It is not clear where the poet stands. Nor where lies the blame for the falling-away described: at Gladstone's door or elsewhere, for blame is certainly being implied. We have an idea of the poet's attitude from his review in October 1918 of Lytton Strachey's *Eminent Victorians*: 'It is, indeed, difficult to restrain one's growing conviction that Mr. Gladstone was not all his party had hoped for.' And further on: 'but Gladstone was decidedly unpleasant'. Now this is still ambiguous, but the meaning, if not ironical and turned against the party is, we take it, that Gladstone was not as good, or reformist, as the party would have liked. But this is not really conveyed by the poem, which is marred by the uncertainty.

Or take the first poem of part two of *Mauberley*. It means that Mauberley is a Pier Francesca lacking the latter's force and vitality. A Pisanello without Pisanello's ability to re-create the medallic art of ancient Greece. But what it could mean—what the words sometimes seem to say—is that Mauberley, like Pier Francesca, is colourless. And, like Pisanello, unable to 'forge Achaia'. The first interpretation is, I am sure, the right one. But the evidence on which our certainty rests is not in the poem. It is put together with the aid of his other writings, his conversation and a knowledge of his library.

There is good poetry in which ambiguity of primary or surface meaning is irrelevant because the work is controlled by tone and sustained by depth. But Pound's is poetry of surface. And unless the surface has continuity and the tone is strong, the unity suffers. The artist who creates a self-contained world of his own may be allowed wide, though not total, freedom inside that world. Our main concern, at the start, is in making sure that he has created such a world.

II

A DRAFT OF XXX CANTOS 1917–1930

THERE IS no principle of unity visible in these cantos, at least twenty of which suffer from major obscurities. The most we can say is that they bear every sign of Pound's authorship. This is the one unity visible at present. But what is he trying to do? The first 19 lines of canto 3 are about Venice and Tuscany; but the Venetian lines are too personal to have any meaning as they stand, as are the last two of the Tuscan section. Granted, however, that they are about Italy, why are they without explanation placed in the same canto with an incident about Ruy Diaz? What is the connexion in canto 5 between Pieire de Maensac (even if we know who he is—the canto doesn't tell us except in the most cryptic manner) and John Borgia? Canto 6 is mostly about Troubadours, with an implied connexion between sex and artistic creation. But the hint is vague and there is no telling what he really means. What is the connexion, we may ask, in canto 18 between Kublai Khan and the items which follow? We look in vain for the pressure of significance or form which has forced them together into the same canto. The first page of canto 28 contains four separate pieces without any indication of what they have in common, if anything, or why they are there. And so on for another six and a half pages, with nothing tangible to grasp. Not that this is all. The same cantos are full of fine lines and musical passages, apt turns of phrase and remarkable stylistic invention. Our difficulty is that we have no means of knowing where we are, or what we are doing. It does not help much to say that the first canto is a descent

into the underworld. That particular thread gives out some
nine lines before the end of the canto. The Malatesta section,
beginning at canto 8, has a certain unity, so too have the 'Hell'
cantos. But we are conscious for the most part only of an endless
shifting, without anything to hold to, even for a moment, while
we get our bearings. A line understood in isolation is not
necessarily understood in relation to the canto, the section, or
the poem. A passage which pleases is not therefore, on that
account alone, provided with threads which reach out to the
passages surrounding. Skill to please in the short run does not
of itself mean skill to please in the long.

We begin to see that some of the gaps are directly related to
the poet's difficulties with communication. The story of
Poicebot on the second page of canto 5 is inferior to his earlier
prose version in the article 'Troubadours: Their Sorts and
Conditions'. In the canto he leaves out much of the story,
ignoring the story-teller's art. When at any time he succeeds, it
is because he explains what he means:

> And there was that squirt of an Ausstrrian
>   with a rose in his button-hole,
> And how the hell he stayed on here,
>   right through the whole bhloody business,
> Cocky as Kristnoze, and enjoying every Boche victory.
> Naphtha, or some damn thing for the submarines,
> Like they had, just *had*, to have the hemp
>   via Rotterdam.

When he fails to explain, as in the rest of canto 19, the result is a
blank. We cannot say that the result is bad, but neither can we
find any means of entering into it. Impediment and a theory of
condensation, by now ingrained, were raised, thanks to
Fenollosa's intervention, to the status of a philosophy which
placed no limit on, and encouraged, the most extreme formula-
tions. Defects are everywhere to be found. The words in canto 7
beginning 'And the tall indifference moves' are not equal to the
subject matter. Words and subject stand apart. In this case the
words seem too good for the subject. We are unable to match

whatever he is trying to say with the person or persons of which it is being said. The telling in canto 9, on the other hand, is too vague. The recital of incidents from Sigismundo Malatesta's life is monotonous because particular events, unless shot through with universal significance, or brought into collaboration with a world of meaning, are even duller than bad generalizations. The same may be said of canto 16, from 'Gallifet led that triple charge', to the end.

Concentration on style is the best means of ensuring adequate communication. But this presupposes a something to communicate. And it means in practice a certain amount of give and take between style and subject. What seems to have gone wrong in the *Cantos* is this. Instead of achieving tension between the two, Pound concentrates excessively on a single aspect of style, discarding or disfiguring part of his subject in trying to make it conform to the theory that poetry equals condensation, worsening, in other words, the effect of his tendency to leave out essentials by pushing his theory to an extreme. But tendencies and theories aside, we cannot avoid the suspicion that he has not always been as helpful as he might. This applies to political and economic passages especially, and to several dealing with love, sex and the pagan mystery religions. The impression is of information deliberately withheld. But the explanation may once again lie in the poet's psychology. Assuming that he was in possession of the knowledge in the first place, he may have withheld it purposely, speaking only to those capable of penetrating the inner sanctum.

But this account, it will fairly be objected, is unjust because incomplete. For we have said nothing about his use of repetition as a means of continuity. I admit this objection and endorse it for the opportunity it provides to look at this aspect in some detail. What it amounts to basically is this. The same item, or echo thereof, is repeated at irregular intervals, though not always for the same reason or with quite the same meaning. Elpenor who in canto 1 pleads with Odysseus, 'set my oar up that I swung mid fellows,' appears again in canto 20 where we are reminded that most of those who sailed with Odysseus did not have 'their rowing sticks set with Elpenor's'. So-shu, who churns in the sea on the first page of canto 2, uses 'the long moon for churn-stick' a page or two later. The Eleanor who in the same canto is described in Greek as 'destroyer of ships, destroyer of cities' would appear to be Eleanor of Acquitaine, but also Helen of Troy. She is the same woman, or the same type, appearing and reappearing in different historical periods. She is 'De Tierci's wife' and Tyndarida in canto 5; Eleanor, wife of Louis VII and Henry of Anjou, and mother of Richard I, in canto 6; Eleanor and perhaps Helen in 7; and Helen in 8. She is referred to indirectly through the words of the Trojan elders, 'let her go back', in 20. She is De Tierci's wife and Helen in 23, and Helen ('dove fu Elena rapta da Paris') in 24. This notion of woman the destroyer turns up again in the *Pisan Cantos* and later.

Other 'repeats' include: Tyro (cantos 2 and 7); Sordello (2, 6 and 29); the young Pound in Venice (opening lines of 3 and 26, and possibly the 'corner cook-stall' of 4); Ignez de Castro (3 and 30); and the city of Ecbatan (4 and 5). Pound sitting by or in the Roman arena at Verona is touched on in cantos 4, 12, 21 and 29, and perhaps in 11. But whether all refer to the same occasion I am not certain. In canto 29 it is toward sundown *by* the arena. There is one present who has lace at the wrist, and a conversation ensues about the love of death. Turning to the fifth page of canto 78, we find the scene repeated. This time with additional details but without the reference to death. The additional details, however, are of interest. The group is sitting outside the arena. Present, apart from Pound, are at least two others: 'Thiy' and 'il decaduto'. 'Thiy' was Mrs Bride Scratton, the B. M. G. Adams who contributed *England* to the 'Inquest' series of small prose books edited by Pound for the Three Mountains Press in Paris 1923–24. (Other books in the series included Ford Madox Ford's *Women and Men*, Pound's *Indiscretions* and Hemingway's *In Our Time*.) There is nothing upon which to base our identification of 'il decaduto', the decadent one. But immediately afterwards (linked to the rest by a 'but') Pound mentions the literary programme drawn up by Eliot and himself at the Café Dante in Verona, which to his annoyance was ignored by Eliot in editing the *Criterion*. It is noteworthy that Mrs Scratton thought she remembered Eliot placing the *Waste Land* (or part of it perhaps?) before Pound at a café table in Verona. Diligent work upon cantos 29 and 78 might uncover the characters. But it is possible of course that Pound is telescoping several occasions.

Let us return to the 'repeats'. 'O se morisse' of canto 5 is varied slightly in canto 7. The *remir* of canto 7, from Arnaut Daniel's 'E quel remir contral lum de la lampa', is repeated in 20, and the 'Thin husks' of 7 echoed perhaps in the 'Noble forms, lacking life' of 25 and Tovarisch of 27. Alessandro the negro horseman (cantos 8 and 26); a wall 'painted to look like arras' (20 and 23); the Greek 'Ligur' aoide' (twice, canto 20); Pound's grandfather, Thaddeus Coleman Pound, who 'sweated blood to put through that railway' (21, 22 and 28); and Phoibos and the ivory tower (21 and 29). 'Confusion, source of renewals' in 21 is echoed perhaps in 'forms and renewals' in 25. We continue: Phaethusa and the 'smoke-faint throat' (21 and 25); M. Curie (23 and 27); and the birth of Venus (23 and 25). There are quotations from, or references to, Dante in at least the following: 5, 7, 8, 14, 15, 16, 20, 23 and 25.

With one or two possible exceptions these 'repeats' look better isolated than in the poem. They are certainly a lot clearer when woven together into a 'structure' by the critic than in context. They exist and sometimes echo as apparently intended. But it is too early to say whether they give continuity. In the first thirty cantos they do no more than suggest the possibility of continuity later if more fully developed.

But more puzzling, more unexpected than the absence of a grand design, is the fact, often obscured for the enthusiastic reader by the brilliance of the work, that there are numerous weaknesses of music and rhythm. As with music, the movement of verse is at a level of being which links it to the existence of the reader—almost, as it were, to his essence in activity—and cannot be analysed in terms of external sound completely separate from him. This is one reason why handbooks on

14

versification and studies which claim to treat of verse from this point of view usually seem so lifeless. They do not deal with the subject at all. The categories of sound they set before us are not only divorced from words, they fail to be the rhythms and sounds of verse. They remain, at last, random noises and emphases which have no life at the level of being at which poetry operates.

In order to give a just account of rhythm and sound in verse —keeping in mind that no account can be adequate—we must present it not in lifeless pieces but in action while it is about its business as an essential part of poetry. That is what we shall try to do here. Rhythm takes its meaning from the poetry in which it resides: its appreciation therefore is inseparable from the appreciation of the latter. A distinctive note of good rhythm is that it imposes itself, imposes a tone on the reader while at the same time allowing each word its full natural weight on its own or as part of the phrase. This is nowhere clearer than in *The Vanity of Human Wishes* where, contrary to what we might expect, the strictness and orderly movement serve to light up the remarkable extent to which individual word and phrase are allowed the freedom necessary to register their weight.

A further important aspect of verse rhythm not unrelated to this is that it draws its strength from speech and in the end always points back towards speech, no matter how elaborate it may have become or how far it may have departed from some of the more obvious outward appearances of the spoken language. Immersed in the latter, well read in the literature of the past and to a lesser extent of his own time, the poet may concentrate narrowly on the writing of his verse, on the delineation of images, the maintenance of unity, of tone and so forth, without for a moment losing touch with the possibilities and limitations of his medium. When he knows the spoken language and has studied well the poetry of the past, the language both past and present is alive always in his ear telling him of what is in keeping with its ways and warning of the presence of what is not. Despite Pound's feeling for the music and rhythm of verse he was sometimes carried away in the wrong direction by his

own theories and the poetry and theories of his friends. Some
of Ford's early poems are in the same line as *Lustra* and passages in the *Cantos*:

> Come in the delicate stillness of dawn,
> Your eyelids heavy with sleep
> > ('The Face of the Night', 1904)

Pound most likely benefited from Ford's verse, as he says.
But he attributed virtues to the latter's 'On Heaven' which it
did not possess. What he liked about it was the informal and
(as he thought) natural language. But its fault, if compared
with his own work of the period, is that it is loose and easy in
the wrong way, and natural only in so far as it copies a few of
the surface aspects of speech, or an imagined speech, without
taking the sinew of the spoken language into its own being.
This surface naturalness finds its way sometimes into the *Cantos*,
along with imagery and expressions which in his younger days
he might have rejected as sloppy.

And while there are passages of high art in the *Draft* which
reach the lucidity and firmness of parts of the *Pisan Cantos*:

> 'and built a temple so full of pagan works'
> > i.e. Sigismund
> and in the style 'Past ruin'd Latium'
> The filagree hiding the gothic,
> > with a touch of rhetoric in the whole
> And the old sarcophagi,
> > such as lie, smothered in grass, by San Vitale.

and:

> > I saw then, as of waves taking form,
> As the sea, hard, a glitter of crystal,
> And the waves rising but formed, holding their form.
> No light reaching through them.

and feats of rhetoric seldom surpassed in English verse:

> And that he did among other things
> Empty the fonts of the chiexa of holy water
> And fill up the same full with ink

That he might in God's dishonour
Stand before the doors of the said chiexa
Making mock of the inky faithful, they
Issuing thence by the doors in the pale light of the sunrise
Which might be considered youthful levity
    but was really a profound indication;

'Whence that his, Sigismundo's, foetor filled the earth
And stank up through the air and stars to heaven
Where—save they were immune from sufferings—
It had made the emparadisèd spirits pewk' . . .
    from their jeweled terrace.

Yet there are times when the ear fails or the tone falters. Even
a brilliant page like that beginning 'The valley is thick with
leaves' in canto 4, has too much in common for comfort with
bad 'free verse'. Like the sonorous 'Cave of Nerea' passage in
canto 17 it has an air about it of improvisation, of beautiful
pieces strung together without much thought to the overall
effect. But even where passages of ten or twelve lines are successful in themselves, taken as fragments, he is not always able to
round them off, or join them musically to other passages. The
diction is sometimes as sounding almost, and certainly as
strange, as some of Milton's:

    Venerandam,
In the Cretan's phrase, with the golden crown, Aphrodite,
Cypri munimenta sortita est, mirthful, oricalchi, with golden
Girdles and breast bands, thou with the dark eyelids
Bearing the golden bough of Argicida. So that:

But he lacks Milton's power to resolve strangeness and irregular-
ity in the larger rhythm of the paragraph and the narrative.
Pound has variety, vitality, and sense of timing. But he cannot
round off his separate accomplished pieces and relate them to
their surroundings. We are conscious in canto 2 of metamorphosis and the sea, and of lines and short passages of great
beauty, but not of anything fully accomplished—no larger
musical unit brought to a successful conclusion—when we

reach the end of its five pages. And when the tone in the *Cantos* falters, it usually falters badly:

> And he was in the sick wards, and on the high tower
> And everywhere, keeping us at it.
> And, thank God, they got the sickness outside
> As we had the sickness inside,
> And they had neither town nor castello
> But dey got de mos' bloody rottenes' peace on us—
> *Quali lochi sono questi:*
> .Sogliano,
> Torrano and La Serra . . .
>   (canto 11)

It is hard to imagine by what process the line 'But dey got de mos' bloody rottenes' peace on us' was here inserted. It has the effect of calling attention to the poet rather than his subject, in such a way as to make us wonder whether he is as serious about these Malatesta cantos as he pretends to be. It is not a deft touch which suddenly and with great economy lights up a new aspect of the situation, but a tasteless change of tone inserted apparently without reason. Although sometimes Pound has a fine ear for dialect, he seldom succeeds when he tries to weave the voices together:

> And how can yew be here? Why don't the fellers at home
> Take it all off you? How can you leave your big business?
> 'Oh,' he sez, 'I ain't had to rent any money . . .
> 'It's a long time since I ain't had to rent any money.'
> Nawthin' more about Das Kapital,
> Or credit, or distribution . . .
>   (canto 19)

The first four lines are lifeless, but the fifth (Pound's own comment in dialect) and the sixth (his own comment continued but now in a 'neutral' tone) ruin the passage completely. Other examples of this faltering in tone are:

> Where they sent him to do in the Mo'ammeds (canto 11)
> Bored with their bloomin' primness (canto 12)
> place where those men went for the Silk War (canto 16)

'Three hundred men killed in that 'splosion' (canto 18)
Who wuz agoin' to stop him (canto 22)

Each is a false note out of keeping with its surroundings. The playfulness might in other circumstances be justified, but in no case here. Poetic decorum does not limit subject-matter or means of expression, but the when and where of use. Not so strange perhaps that Pound has something in common here with Keats. Wordsworth, who preserved much of the Augustan order and refinement went safely on his own way precisely because he carried a large enough part of his heritage with him, and the ability to use it. Not so always with Keats whose grasp of the previous century, and understanding of his own aims were not so firm. The 'cloudy trophies' of the *Ode to Melancholy* is not, I think, altogether bad in itself. It is possible, at any rate, to think of it as finding a suitable place in a more formal poem. But in the *Ode* it is plumped down in a setting that is foreign to it and no amount of familiarity on our part can bring the two worlds together. The discord between 'sick for home' and 'alien corn' in *Ode to the Nightingale* argues a related uncertainty in the realm of sound. Such a blemish would have been more quickly noticed in Johnson's time when it would certainly have caused more pain. The line, 'Canned beef for Apollo, ten cans for a boat load' in canto 20, displays a similar lack of decorum. In other circumstances maybe, it is a striking figure, but here clashes with every one of the twenty lines it is supposed to resolve. It is not a legitimate contrast, or shock, worked into and made part of, the passage in which it occurs. It is foreign to it, a stray line from a different speech. It is possible perhaps to conceive of a poem in which *ingles, waiting maids* and *seaweed under lightning* peacefully coexist with *canned beef*; but this is not it. It is one more curious example of a line which seemed 'creative' and vital when it first appeared becoming dated in less than fifty years. *Prufrock* marks a period. It will never be possible to think in future of Edwardian days without it. 'Canned beef for Apollo', on the other hand, is an unsuccessful scrap of Jazz Age 'modernism'.

I have tried to exhibit the impact of the first thirty cantos in as fair a manner as possible. If I have found fault more often than I have praised, it is because the difficulties seem to me excessive, in what is, after all, no mere preliminary flourish but almost a third of the poem. One-third, without the poet having given us any firm directions about how to read the work, or produced anything in the way of structure or continuity, beyond several hints which do not stand up under examination. One exception perhaps is the Eleanor figure, 'destroyer of men, destroyer of cities'. But most of the other 'repeats' seem commonplace, of no structural validity. And while it may be difficult to define exactly what we mean by poetic unity there is legitimate ground for refusing to admit its presence so far in the *Cantos*.

If we summarize, this is what we find. First a descent into the Homeric underworld, possibly metaphorical. Metamorphosis and the sea in canto 2, suggesting perhaps a kind of permanence underlying change. Next, an appearance of the author in Venice for two or three lines, in canto 3, after which he makes occasional appearances throughout. We have at least four blocks of historical material all dealing with medieval or Renaissance Italy: (1) a highly stylized portrait of Sigismundo Malatesta (cantos 8 to 11); (2) the Medici family (cantos 5, 7, 8, 21 and 26); (3) the Este family (cantos 20 and 24); and (4) Venice (cantos 25 and 26). Probably the most effective is that dealing with Sigismundo, which should be compared with the prose summary in Chapter 24 of *Guide to Kulchur*. There is a contrast in canto 26 which seems to say that artists were better off in Renaissance Italy than was Mozart under a particular Archbishop of Salzburg. Several other cantos deal with fraud, and there is a 'Hell' mainly for Londoners, which illustrates Pound's blindness to reality but is a *tour de force* nevertheless. There are suggestions here and there of a pagan paradise, and dozens of items ranging from a few words to a page which may represent the transient as it passes.

But these points are much easier to follow here than in the poem where they are in no visible order, held together by no visible principle. Even the mildest interpretation finds no clear warrant in the text. And what aggravates a suspicion that the *Draft* may be fragmentary in fact and not just in appearance is the unsatisfactory music. His failure to resolve the separate musical units and join them together may not be unconnected with the breakdown in other dimensions. The idea has been seriously entertained of the *Cantos* as a fugue, but this seems inept. A more suitable analogy perhaps is Wagnerian opera. The *Cantos* may be seen as an unsuccessful attempt to apply Wagner to poetry. There is no evidence I know of that Pound had Wagner in mind when planning the work, but an investigation of his association with the pianist and composer Walter Morse Rummel in Paris about 1911 might yield a different answer.

III

NUEVO MUNDO 1934

THIS SECTION is political and historical, interrupted twice by cantos on love and sex. The *Draft XXX of Cantos* ends with the death of a Borgia pope in the early sixteenth century. 'Nuevo Mundo' opens with Thomas Jefferson. Since the poem is not moving chronologically it is probably safe to assume that there is no significance in the gap of nearly three centuries.

Earlier appearances of the New World were mostly concerned with fraud and money-making. Now, with Jefferson, John Adams, John Quincy Adams and Martin Van Buren, we are among the just law-givers. The contrast with the rulers of Europe is strongly drawn. Jefferson is master of all situations, equally at home in politics, science, art. Louis the Sixteenth, on the other hand, is a fool, the King of Spain a fool, the King of Naples a fool, the King of Sardinia 'like all the Bourbons' a fool, the Portuguese Queen a fool, the successor to Frederic of Prussia a mere hog, Gustavus and Joseph of Austria crazy and George the Third in a straight waistcoat. If it is like a play in which the hero has all the good lines and the rest say nothing or are conspicuously foolish, it is because Pound has accommodated himself to a view of the American founders which makes this easy. It is not for us to question this view at this stage. We must see first whether he succeeds in turning it into poetry.

The opening page of canto 31 establishes the desired note. Jefferson, we learn immediately, is a man of affairs: one moment writing to Washington about water communication with the western country, the next arranging for Tom Paine's passage to America in a public vessel, or discussing slavery or a flower 'that vegetates when suspended in air'. This note is maintained, successfully I should say, throughout. But when canto 32 goes on in the same vein, the Americans looking down with godlike detachment upon a world populated by fools, nonentities or worse, we realize that a straightforward judgment of the poetry, without reference to the history, is not as easy as we thought. The Americans are so honest, so intelligent, so full of common sense, the rest so utterly incompetent or dishonest, that we immediately look for the irony. But there is none. Pound's world *is* populated thus. 'Mr Jefferson' and 'Mr Adams' comprehend the world as in a nutshell and act accordingly; the Emperor Franz Josef is 'that lousy old bewhiskered sonvabitch . . . of whom nothing good is recorded'. This is Pound's world and we must accept it for the sake of the poem; but not absolutely. We cannot hope to read this kind of poetry intelligently while pretending that the meaning doesn't matter or that the poet's views are totally irrelevant. The idea that we should read poetry for the sake of the poetry and not something else is important as critical discipline and sometimes very useful against a certain type of bad criticism. But it is not a detachable gadget to be applied when and where we like. We must take into account Pound's complete lack of understanding of human beings and the human heart, even if— as in the case of the rulers of Europe during the eighteenth and nineteenth centuries—such understanding is not part of his purpose.

Some excerpts from letters in cantos 31 and 32 are too brief to make sense, but serve, I suppose, to illustrate the wide range of Jefferson's mind and his ability to switch from one thing to another without losing his grip. Other extracts make sense but are puzzling. When he gives to John Adams the lines:

'. . . wish that I cd. subjoin Gosindi's Syntagma
'of the doctrines of Epicurus.'

does he mean only that Adams was well read, or are we to take it more seriously, as containing some philosophical implication? The former seems the most likely, but the method is so uncertain that we may have looked into the argument between Descartes and Gassendi over the logical sense of *Cogito ergo sum* or made enquiries about Gassendi's *Animadversiones in decem libri Diogenis Laertii*, the third edition 1675, with an appendix containing 'Philosophia Epicuri Syntagma', before realizing that it has nothing to do with the *Cantos*.

Canto 33 contains some thirty extracts from the writings of Adams, Jefferson, Marx, Senator Brookhart and others, placed one after the other without any comment or assistance. Some are immediately interesting, and the first, a statement by John Adams on the corruption of history, a guide perhaps to Pound's own thought on the subject, as we shall see later. But why some are quoted at all, or why these extracts and not thirty others, is far from obvious. The meaning, if we take a hint from the descriptions of nineteenth-century industrial life, is that the capitalist system is bad. But how bad ultimately, and compared with what, he doesn't say; it is left in the air. The extracts at the end dealing with the Federal Reserve banks are, I believe, from a speech in 1930 or 1931 by Senator Smith Brookhart, of the Committee on Interstate Commerce. Pound corresponded with him in March and April 1931 about a speech in which the Senator criticized Eugene Meyer's direction of the Federal Reserve system. Pound's letter of 18 March 1931 begins: 'Your speech against Meyer (Congressional Record 28 February, p. 6598) seems to me very important. Parts of it at any rate seem to me the most important historical document of the period I have come upon.'

Canto 34 is composed of extracts from the Diary of John Quincy Adams. The meaning is clear, so long as we ask no more than a rough idea of a man mixing in affairs and jotting down his observations. Canto 35 is devoted to Central Europe. The anecdotes and comments are at times cleverly phrased, though once again we are not always sure what meaning Pound wishes us to draw. The lines about the 'Fraulein Doktor' refer to the division of the Tyrol, the northern part remaining with Austria, the southern part going to Italy, after the First World War; and those about the 'high cheek bones' to the racial background of some East European Jews who are sometimes said to be descended from a Mongol tribe which settled in or near Hungary in the Dark Ages. The sudden switch to Mantuan trade regulations may be designed to illustrate the sharp contrast he sees between Central Europe and Italy. The passage beginning 'When the stars fall from the olive' and the reference to Venice are too condensed to yield any real meaning. The question ' "Victoria? Where 'ave I 'eard that nyme?" ' is taken from a cartoon by Max Beerbohm. Maybe it is placed next to business details of fifteenth-century Venice because Pound sees a connexion between the maritime Republic and the commercial life of Victorian England.

Sandwiched between Central Europe and President Van Buren is canto 36, containing a translation of Cavalcanti's 'Donna mi prega' and some observations on sex, art and clear thinking. After 25 pages dealing mainly with the early United States, nineteenth-century industrial conditions, and Central Europe of fifty or fewer years ago, we are suddenly confronted with a thirteenth-century Italian love poem, translated by Pound into a strangely compelling English. No introduction of any sort, no line or two about why, just the poem. And when, in search of Pound's attitude to Cavalcanti and the 'Donna mi prega', we consult his essay 'Cavalcanti', we find nothing there that throws light on our problem. Left to our own devices we decide first of all that it is a contrast: Cavalcanti representing medieval clarity, against the emotional chaos of Mitteleuropa, as Pound calls it. And we may grant this within the *Cantos*, even if outside it we regard his portrait of Central Europe as inadequate and his view of Cavalcanti too highly personal. For the 'Donna mi prega" while it does not illustrate medieval lucidity and psychological subtlety as well as the *Vita Nuova*, does on the other hand give us an insight into a medieval way of mind, and the Mitteleuropa of canto 35, while only a caricature, serves perhaps to bring this out.

Secondly, there is the question of canto 36 as a possible key to the underlying nature of the whole work. It does not serve the same apparently metaphorical purpose as the long extract from Homer in canto 1, or the two pages from Hanno's *Periplus* in canto 40. It is a direct statement about love, followed immediately by references to clear thought, coition and the troubadour Sordello. Remembering canto 6 with its suggestion of a ritual connexion between coition and song, we may feel that here at last we are in sight of a link that will do more than connect; that will explain. The reference to 'thrones' (see *Paradiso*, IX) immediately after the 'Donna mi prega' may mean that we are now in or near paradise. After which follow some thirty lines I interpret thus. Scotus Erigena who said 'Authority comes from right reason, never the other way on', was a great thinker ahead of his time. He was condemned (post mortem) after a search for Manichaeans in Provence, presumably conducted by men like Aquinas ('head down in a vacuum') and Aristotle ('not quite in a vacuum'), both of whom show up poorly against Erigena. All this and the words 'Sacrum, sacrum, inluminatio coitu' which follow, are meant to suggest a connexion between Erigena and the troubadours: the existence of a common source of ideas, or even of an underground mystery religion in which the knowledge derived from coition was held to be sacred. Then comes the reference to Sordello whose love for Cunizza, wife of Richard St Boniface, is celebrated in canto 6 (and in the essay 'Troubadours—Their Sorts and Conditions'). The canto ends with Sordello's line: 'Quan ben m'albir e mon ric pensamen' ('When I consider well in my rich thought'). The interlude about 'Charles the Mangy of Anjou' may be in illustration of the king's magnanimity.

We still cannot be sure that we have here one of the basic ideas on which the poem depends. But considering the many earlier references to love and the troubadours, we would appear to be on the right track. Canto 36, we may allow; is a step towards crystallization of an idea previously hinted at. It in no sense explains the earlier cantos, nor unravels the many problems we have encountered; but it does supply the hope of reaching later a stable vantage-point from which to view the rest. The need for such is apparent as soon as we turn to canto 37. For then we are back in the early United States, transcribing extracts from the Autobiography of Martin Van Buren.

Pound first received definite information about the Autobiography in a letter dated 29 March 1932 from a friend in New York State. He obtained a copy later that year, and had written canto 37 by 14 September 1933, for at that date we find him urging Harriet Monroe to publish it as soon as possible in *Poetry*. Any hesitation on her part was understandable, for while it contains amusing observations:

> Shall we call in the world to conduct our
> municipal government?

the canto as a whole could not but appear strange, or even pointless, to one who had not read the Van Buren or given a week or two to the study of the period. The Autobiography was written about 1860 at Sorrento, with Van Buren looking back on the early and middle years of a long and eventful political life which culminated in the presidency 1837–41. The manuscript was apparently kept in the family after his death in 1862 until about 1905, when a manuscript copy by his son, who was his literary executor, was presented by some later member of the family to the Library of Congress. It was published in Washington in 1920 as volume two of the Annual Report of the American Historical Association for 1918.

Pound skims through it taking out bits that interest him, anything especially that has to do with the struggle between President Jackson and the Second Bank of the United States. Since he is quick-witted the results of his skimming are often pointed, but hardly history. The Autobiography itself is not the last word by any means on Van Buren's political life. And if, further, we take into account the fact that Pound's eyes were at this stage guided by certain reformist attitudes (cantos 12 14, 15, 16, 17, 18, 22 and 33) we will understand why canto 37, like his portrait of Sigismundo earlier, is lacking in essentials where historical balance is concerned. What we are getting of course are not real men but Ezra Pound's heroes. There is no sign in 37 of Van Buren the professional—who is sometimes credited with having invented the modern political machine—as, in the Malatesta cantos, there is no proper coverage of the less savoury aspects of Sigismundo's life. For example: the line in canto 9, 'And there was the row about that German-Burgundian female', does not indicate that 'the row' included an unsolved murder. The fact that Pound wants us to regard his history as real, and not just the elaboration of a moral world, does indeed raise problems, especially in an age as conscious of historical perspective as our own. But there is no way at present but to accept these histories for the sake of the poem and hope for some resolution later.

Canto 37 by the way contains an interesting lapse in communication. Brief mention of a Washington social scandal in Van Buren's time, 'Peggy Eaton's Own Story', is followed immediately by this:

> And if Marietta
> Had not put on her grandmother's dress
> She might have lasted, a mystery even. If Dolores
> Had not put on a hat shaped like a wig
> She might have remained an exotic.
> Placuit oculis, and did not mind strong cigars.

Forty-four cantos, or 361 pages later, we discover (if we still remember at all) that Pound met Dolores in Spain, *c.* 1906:

> and Dolores said: Come pan, niño, eat bread, me lad
> Sargent had painted her
> (canto 81)

This then enables us to go back 26 pages to the first page of canto 80, where 'Come pan, niño' is quoted without mention of Dolores. And to enjoy the sensation of discovery (provided of course that it is the same Dolores), even if we are still none the wiser about her connexion with Peggy Eaton or Van Buren. The local meaning perhaps is that Sargent might not have painted her, or Pound remembered, if she had not put on the hat shaped like a wig.

Much of canto 38 seems to be in the same vein of unexplained reminiscence. Fragments of conversation or reading that are beyond us at the moment. Or, if not beyond us, annoying, as in the case of the line ' "And God take your living" said Hawkwood', which depends upon our knowing either the original story or Pound's footnote on page 70 of *Spirit of Romance*, 1953 edition. We understand a number of passages in a general way: the author does not like brokers or gun-sellers; he has an obsession about Central Europe, which makes him like one of his own Central European characters; Mr Blodgett was wrong when he said that 'Sewing machines will never come into general use'; and gun-sellers sell guns and only ever do good in order to do evil. But we get tired of cryptic utterances implying meaning and depth without providing any. The 25 lines beginning ' "I have of course never said" ' are an attempt to put into a simple statement C. H. Douglas's 'A plus B theorem' in which the latter explains the deficiency of the present price system and establishes a basis for the issue of national dividends. The lines may be clear in themselves, but not as part of the canto. We see why the theorem follows Mr Blodgett: like the sewing-machine it will eventually come into its own, despite the Blodgetts among economists. But what is its connexion with Krupp and Schneider? Pounds warns:

> the light became so bright and so blindin'
> in this layer of paradise
> that the mind of man was bewildered.

But he does not attempt to help us on our way. I have a feeling, which may or may not be shared by others who have gone more deeply into the subject, that he did not at this stage have the necessary knowledge to draw the material together. If it be argued that this was not his intention, that he was engaged in something quite different, I am, I confess, still in the dark. And when I read through the canto again looking for possible clues I end more firmly convinced than before that it is spurious.

The line, 'Mr Mellon went over to England', is a good example. It hints at inside information, but says nothing.

We note that in canto 38, first published in September 1933, he refers to the German anthropologist Leo Frobenius ('The white man who made the tempest in Baluba'), who from this time on was increasingly praised by Pound, in his prose particularly. I have not been able to discover when first he began reading Frobenius, but he had correspondence with a Viennese bookshop in February 1930 about buying the seven-volume *Erlebte Erdteile* and the separately published *Paideuma*.

With canto 39 we are back with coition. Parts are excellent and if one of the intentions of the first two pages is to give off an aura of sex as physical pleasure, a blind need and a release, then probably it succeeds. The Odysseus episode may mean that the hero clears his mind and gains knowledge by copulating with Circe: an echo of 'Sacrum, sacrum, inluminatio coitu' in canto 36. The second part of the canto beginning 'Sumus in fide' is a chant to Venus and conception, but more ritualistic than the earlier and more definitely connected, I should say, in Pound's mind with the Eleusinian mysteries.

It is easy to claim, as I have heard it done, that this is one of the key cantos. It is beautiful certainly, but disjointed, and there is once again the problem of overall meaning and the author's refusal to explain himself or give directions. What for example is the meaning or purpose of the Hathor passage? If it is the Egyptian Hathor, why has he changed the story? Or if it is another Hathor, or perhaps the Egyptian one received via a North African tradition, and recorded in Frobenius—why doesn't he tell us? Once again we suspect he may be trying to imply more than he knows or more than he is able to turn into poetry. We ought also to mention in passing a failure in diction: 'Been to hell in a boat yet?', which once perhaps seemed fresh and 'modern', but is interesting now mainly as a museum-piece.

The first two pages of canto 40 deal mainly with American business and finance, from 1858 until the Pujo Investigation early in the present century. They are clear enough in a general

way, so long as we have handy the *Annotated Index*. The 'Mr
Corey' listed there as William Ellis Corey the American
industrialist may possibly be the Marxist historian Lewis Corey
whose book on J. P. Morgan, and one other, on American
capitalism, Pound was reading about the time he wrote this
canto. Half way through he breaks off suddenly from the world
of bankers and 'unreadable books bound in tree-calf' to go
with Hanno on a Carthaginian voyage of discovery to the
Atlantic coast of North Africa, a voyage which ends apparently
in 'the empyrean . . . the ineffable crystal'. This may be the
realm of the heroes or just law-givers, for canto 41 opens
immediately afterwards with Mussolini:

> 'Ma questo,'
> said the Boss, 'è divertente.'
> catching the point before the aesthetes had got there . . .

It is not clear what Mussolini finds so entertaining: maybe the
consortium mentioned a few lines further on, but more likely
the *Cantos*. The meaning then would be that Mussolini caught
the point of the poem before the litterati. The canto would seem
to depict, on the one hand the early struggles and rule of
Mussolini the intelligent ruler who drained the marshes, etc.,
and, on the other, the worn-out ruling class or classes of the
rest of Europe. This is followed by cryptic reference to a good
bank (Monte dei Paschi), and a good money system (Woergl),
some observations by Jefferson on taxation and banking and a
few lines at the end on the manufacture of armaments. The
deficiencies of canto 41 are those already dealt with, and it
would serve no useful purpose to dwell further on particular
cases.

I have thought it more likely to assist the reader if before
attempting a summary of 'Nuevo Mundo', I list some of the
'repeats' within the section and others going back to the first
thirty cantos. First, within the section. Jefferson on tobacco and
taxation, canto 31, is repeated in 41, and 'Gun barrels, black
walnut . . .', mentioned twice in 34, may be connected with
' "The wood (walnut) will always be wanted for gunstocks",'

in 38. The Tyrol, Franz Josef and ' "We find the land over-brained" ' appear in 35 and again in 38, C. H. Douglas in 38 and 41, Mr D'Arcy in 38 and 40, and Circeo in 39 and 41. ' "Peggy Eaton's own story" ' occurs twice in 37 and there are a number of references through the section to Bonaparte, Jackson and Adams.

Links with the first thirty cantos include: Jefferson, first mentioned in canto 21, who is taken up again in detail in 31; Sordello, cantos 2, 6 and 16 ('the light as after a sun-set', *Purgatorio*, VIII) who is taken up again in 32 ('a guisa de leon ... quando si posa', *Purgatorio*, VI) and also 36; and 'that son of a bitch, Franz Josef of Austria', who, introduced in canto 16, is brought in again in 35 and 38. Metevsky (cantos 18 and 38), Odysseus (1, 39, etc.), Venice (26, 40, etc.), Messire Uzano (21 and 41) and coition (6, 36 and 39).

Taken in the round 'Nuevo Mundo' looks like a continuation of the *Draft of XXX Cantos*. The Jefferson section is more compact, less detailed, perhaps, than the much longer Sigismundo section earlier, but seems to serve the same purpose of showing a cultured ruler in the act of ordering events. Other heroes in 'Nuevo Mundo' are John Adams, John Quincy Adams, Martin Van Buren, Andrew Jackson and Mussolini. Over against these, though not with the clarity and definition that this implies, we see chaos and worse: 'child labour', 'the African slave trade', 'Mitteleuropa', 'damned jews in exile', 'Krupp cannon', a bank 'deranging the country's credits', and so on. Let us assume, for a moment, that this contrast is firmly established and that we see the just rulers drawing order out of the sea of chaos and evil which surrounds them. Where does this get us with regard to the work as a whole? There are parallels, of course, between 'Nuevo Mundo' and the *Draft*, not very striking but clear enough for us to believe with a fair degree of certainty that they were intended as such by the author. Thus Jefferson is the equivalent in 'Nuevo Mundo' of Sigismundo in the *Draft*, and the chaos and evil, mentioned above, of the earlier fraud and 'Hell'. But the most we can allow, even so, is that 'Nuevo Mundo' is a continuation of the first section, a prolongation of the introduction well into the body of the poem. There is no sense of advance, no emergence of structure, unless we except cantos 36 and 39 which may be said to develop the coition idea of canto 6 and to introduce a philosophical notion of sorts, which later may enable us to see the poet's world, not yet visible to us as a consistent entity, through the frame of his views on sex, creativity, and clear thought.

But even the contrast we assumed is not firmly established, it is no more than hinted at, and the poet still refuses to explain himself or say by what light he is guided. There are those, I believe, who see in the *Cantos* a consistent attitude amounting to a design, but this is by no means evident to us all. In the first two hundred of the work's eight hundred pages we have come across numerous items repeated, but this, we submit, does not amount to design unless the 'repeats' convey meaning; and, what is more, meaning compounded. It may be of course our quest that is at fault. We may be looking for the wrong thing. Pound may be holding the work together, creating a form, by some new means to which we who think in more or less traditional categories are blind. This is a possibility we will have to keep in view. Meanwhile, here is a point which makes us wonder whether we are not right in supposing that Pound is trying to be, as well as poet, an historian in the modern sense. Note first that in canto 37 and throughout he adheres rigidly to the idea that the struggle between Jackson and the Second Bank was between the people on the one hand, and the banks and their congressional henchmen on the other. Yet in canto 37 he quotes, from, I think, Van Buren's Autobiography, the lines:

> merchants will not confess over trading
>   nor speculators the disposition to speculate . . .

which, if pursued, might well lead us to decide that the so-called bank war was not so clear cut after all, and that the monetary troubles of the time were as much due to the greed and desires of 'the people' as to manipulation by bankers. What has happened, probably, is this. Pound, in skimming through the Autobiography has noted an interesting point about the history of the time and included it in his canto. The reader will see our difficulty immediately. Van Buren is one of the heroes, one of the just law-givers, who was on the side of the people against the Second Bank. But here, sticking awkwardly out from this supposedly self-contained world, are two lines—and there are others—which if followed up might destroy it altogether. We may prove to be wrong of course. The lines may in time be found to be consistent with the world of the heroes. But how do we know until we investigate?

This does not warrant further discussion at the moment. Nor do I wish to submerge the poetry beneath a flurry of questions about history. But what does need saying is that it was Pound who created the situation in the first place. It was he who insisted on writing about history in a way that appears historical rather than poetical. We may be wrong, but that is how it appears. More important still, however, is the fact that there are numerous passages, some quite long, which cannot be understood unless we already have a fair knowledge of the works read or skimmed by Pound in his historical researches.

The most I wish to maintain at this juncture is that it is necessary in reading the *Cantos* to make reservations about the history, which, while they may not altogether spoil, certainly lessen, our enjoyment of the poetry. If comparisons will aid, let us look at Saint John Perse's *Anabasis*. It, too, is a poem including history. But we notice the difference immediately. He has subjected the history to the poem, and it is the poetic unity that is paramount. Everything: tone, story, images are turned into poetry. And if, tomorrow, all the history on which it is based is found to be defective, the clay tablets wrongly interpreted, or the whole formed out of a mistaken identification of several periods and places, our reading of it will not be affected in the slightest, for the Stranger, the City, the sights, smells and sounds, formed by the poet out of history and human activity, are real now at another level of being.

IV

THE FIFTH DECAD 1937

WE SEE HERE, for the first time clearly, that the *Cantos* is a passionate effort to make sense out of history and current events, and to reconcile chaos and evil with the order and design of the Creator. An attempt, let us say, to justify the ways of God to man. The sole unity we could find, which we described rather vaguely earlier as due to the presence of a single author, is now explained. It is, quite simply, unity wrought by a strong enough desire for something to be so.

If we are asked 'But what caused this effort of combination and comprehension to issue in so strange a result?' the more we consider the more difficult we find it to answer: without, that is, going into questions which might be considered too far removed from Pound's own intentions or irrelevant for the world today. But there is another way, not fully reliable, never conclusive, which may, however, give us some idea of the local cause, of how it happened in just the way it did, even if not why. I mean an examination of what he was reading, what he was thinking about, in so far as this is available to us, and what he was writing about in his journalism and letters, while composing the *Cantos*.

Although here we are thinking mainly of the *Fifth Decad* the result if we turned to any other section would be much the same. Knowledge, we find, is being treated like gold. Something to be located, dug for, extracted and shipped. This attitude, which was no more at first than a tendency curbed largely by circumstances, by 1935 had become a fixed habit luxuriously indulged in. We need only mention the attempts to parcel up reality and knowledge into a single convenient bundle, easy for the man moving, the man with his wits about him, to sling over his shoulder; the attempts to make compact solutions to all manner of problems; and the belief that just about anything would yield up its secret to a modicum of practical good sense.

In all this he was very much a man of his time. For his habit was at root the common one of treating all knowledge as something to be acquired by the automatic process of research, and then manipulated, as driver manipulates car, towards some equally tangible and no-nonsense end. Try hard as he did he was never able to grasp fully that we become a thing by knowing it and that the higher the knowledge the more intensely we must live it in the mind in order to understand it. Metaphysical truths were not something arrived at after difficulty and love by the author and understood after love and submission by the reader. They were simply right, wrong, or, what was more likely, hopelessly irrelevant. The metaphysics of India, with all they tell us about the longings of the human spirit, he was thus able to dismiss without having read, as a 'lusting after vacuity'.

It is true, as I have pointed out elsewhere, that some of the calmest of the cantos were written while his mind, if gauged by his articles and letters, was in a serious state of upset. But that is not quite what I refer to above. For while it may have been possible for him to keep the emotions and distractions of his day-to-day politics and economics out of some of the cantos, it does not follow that this therefore applies to all.

Let us go back to 1911. It was about this time that he first met A. R. Orage, editor of the *New Age*, and came under the influence of Allen Upward, who, by putting forward the suggestion that 'intelligence' should be organized into a guild, provided a connecting link between Orage's Guild Socialism and Pound's own aspirations on behalf of the arts. Also important was his meeting with C. H. Douglas in the *New Age* office about 1918, and the latter's formulation not long after of the theory that the present production system produces prices faster than it distributes the power to buy (canto 38). Add to these encounters the following: his talks with Marmaduke Pickthall who had had political experience in Turkey; articles in the *New Age* on political assassination and the recession of power away from the people into the hands of 'inner cliques'; the unsuccessful attempt by Douglas and Orage to interest the Labour Party in Douglas's theories; Orage's attack on Versailles as setting the stage for another world war; and a series of unfortunate experiences—some real, some romanticized, and one at least that was purely hypothetical on Pound's part—with the prevailing publishing system, and what would now, I suppose, be called the Establishment. The result, as we may well imagine, was the desire for a radical shake-up, a new order.

Jump forward a decade or more, to 1935, and we find him now thoroughly immersed in political journalism and the practical details of running various monetary reform movements. One group he supported in many ways ranging from mention in articles to private advice was John Hargrave's Green Shirt Movement, the immediate forebears of which were Kibbo Kift, founded in 1920 'to counteract the ill-effects of industrialism' by encouraging boys to take up woodcraft and hiking, and Douglas's Social Credit. It came into being with the London Hunger March of 30 October 1932. Three years later when Hargrave seemed to be gathering force, Pound helped with the composition of marching songs, donated a flag (embroidered by the Movement with the poet's name), and dedicated his pamphlet *Social Credit: An Impact* 'To the Green Shirts of England'. But at the same time he was involved with a dozen other complementary or conflicting branches of monetary reform. Anyone who seemed to be 'on the move' could command his time, advice and public support, and many others received all three without asking. A letter to John Cournos about the possibility of the Communists in Russia adopting Douglas; another to Harriet Monroe of *Poetry* asking correction of a contributor's statement about money; others to Texas to a small paper devoted to the German reformer Gesell, to Canada where the Alberta experiment was under way, and to an

Anglican clergyman in Queensland, Australia, about the Church's attitude to reform. This, month by month, together with his other work, often left him exhausted and where patient enquiry was needed caused him to look more and more for short cuts.

> I strongly suggest [he wrote to Henry Swabey] you make a study of ecclesiastical money in England. Not numismatism; but to know what the Church issued, under what regulations; ratio metal value to currency value. . . .

The 'Not numismatism' is significant. He wanted the knowledge without the discipline and detail: knowledge on the cheap. But a subject like 'ecclesiastical money' depends upon the detailed labelling and cataloguing of the numismatist. Indeed, all our knowledge of history depends upon specialists like the numismatist whose care with immediate and sometimes apparently inconsequential detail in one generation becomes the basis of wider judgment in the next. This is something which Pound, in common with many others, was apt to forget: what we call significant detail is not in its natural state labelled and waiting for us, it has somehow to be located among a thousand other details of possibly equal significance.

In the four years from 1933 until the publication of the *Fifth Decad*, he produced, in addition to his enormous correspondence, more than four hundred articles and letters-to-the-editor on monetary reform and politics. And while repetition fills a good deal of this space, and the quality is thin, the energy spent must have been considerable. No wonder F. V. Morley of Faber & Faber (for it was Morley and not Eliot who dealt with Pound) was forced to a certain diplomacy to extract literary material from an author reluctant at this stage to write about anything but Douglas and Gesell. Although he could meet bluntness with bluntness when necessary, Morley's lightheartedness and humour delighted Pound and possibly on a number of occasions prevented him from taking his business elsewhere. A typical step in the process by which *Make It New* was born was Morley's assuring the poet that not only had Eliot made a veritable fortune out of *Selected Essays* but was in line for a Bishopric as well.

This survey might naturally be pursued into greater detail, but it is sufficient for us here to have a general idea of the extent of his activity at this time, before passing on to consider its relation to the poem. There is a limit to what any person can do and do well. For myself, I am convinced that in the four years before the *Fifth Decad* appeared, Pound must often have been giving more time and energy to politics and economics than he could afford. He was not a good journalist, except in choosing titles and headings, but he took his journalism very seriously as far as the urgency of it was concerned. So that while there is evidence that much of it was rattled off as fast as he could type, the reading involved, even if only cursory, the thought and the execution cannot be regarded as anything but central to his personality at the time. He was not filling in an odd half-hour left free from poetry and criticism; he was trying to save Europe and America. And this shows in the tone and style of the articles. He was sure, for example, that fear was responsible for the *Morning Post*'s refusal to publish details of the founding of the Monte dei Paschi bank in the seventeenth century:

> If the great daily papers of London DARE NOT publish the history of the Monte dei Paschi . . .

Only a person already living in a world of his own, populated by his own inventions, could draw such a conclusion in such a way. Or take the article ' "We Have Had No Battles but We Have All Joined In and Made Roads" '. The opening refers to the title thus:

> I take this line from a letter of Capt. Goldoni's to indicate the new *forma mentis* with a date line 1935.

Two steps are needed before we can understand this as Pound did. First, Captain Goldoni was serving with the Italian forces in Abyssinia: he apparently mentioned in a letter home that there was no fighting going on at the time, but that they were busy building roads. We must then see that for Pound the road-building and 'we have all joined in' were sure signs of the constructive community spirit of Fascism. He was so wrapped up in his own desires for a better world that the desires had become reality; and, if reality, there was no reason why others should not see them as well.

It is not the ideology with which I am concerned, but the state of mind. Some of what he had to say was no doubt true, but most of it was too general to be of any use without the reader's giving more time to it than the author, and too shrill for any but a convinced monetary reformer to be bothered with anyway. The article 'Twelve Years and Twelve Years' published in the *British-Italian Bulletin* during the 'Abyssinian Crisis' is a good example. He wanted to explain the Italian position and began by presenting his own credentials as an impartial observer:

> Twelve years I lived in London; four years in Paris, and twelve have I lived in Italy, each time from my own free choice. I deny an American Editor's statement that I represent the Italian point of view. If my point of view is not international and organic or structural, I believe that no international point of view can exist, or that there are very few men who can claim it with greater right.
>
> Over twenty years ago, Rabindranath Tagore said apropos of my efforts to bring greater precision into language: 'A patriot is bound to be unpopular. He is always trying to save his country from that which is killing it.' I believe my series of letters appearing in the 'Morning Post' at various dates from Sept. 3rd of last year to Sept. 17th this year contained the maximum of fidelity to England possible for a friend and a foreigner.

So far so good. This is worth reading whether we agree or not. The next paragraph may or may not be connected with what has gone before; the connexion is certainly not brought out:

> I can only reaffirm my belief that Empires decay at the top and in the middle, and that the place to regenerate or cure an Empire is at home. That is what I mean when I say my point of view is organic.

This, we suspect, refers to the British Empire, not the Italian, for as far as Pound was concerned Fascism had already cured Italy at home. And being cured there was free apparently to expand in Abyssinia. Otherwise we might feel that he was simply disregarding the evidence immediately in front of him, namely that the Italians seemed to be doing in Abyssinia precisely the opposite of what he was recommending—attempting a regeneration at the periphery rather than the centre. But the real disclosure follows immediately after. He jumps without warning to usury, because all ills may be traced to the same source:

> I believe that usury is the root of ruin, of decay, of all scarcity economics.
> Europe has lost the distinction between usura and partaggio, usury and fair sharing, yet by this latter you can carry on all commerce, and all manufacture.
> I believe that the men now crying out for the starving and, as they call it, 'sanctioning' of Italy represent the same errors, the same weaknesses of mind that have caused the 'sanctioning' of great masses of the English and French and American population.

My point, to which all this has been leading, is that this was the Pound who wrote the *Fifth Decad*. And while sometimes the poetry wins, and even hysteria is transformed, there is nevertheless a fatal element of unresolved propaganda:

> in hell's bog, in the slough of Vienna, in
>   the midden of Europe in the black hole of all
> mental vileness, in the privvy that stank Franz Josef,
> in Metternich's merdery in the absolute rottenness,
> among embastardized cross-breeds

* * *

> In their soul was usura and in their minds darkness
> and blankness, greased fat were four Georges
> Pus was in Spain, Wellington was jew's pimp
> and lacked mind to know what he effected.

This indeed is the shrill voice of the modern world positing a hell which gains nothing in intelligibility by being brought into relation with its heaven. Compare canto 45 in which the propaganda is part of the poetry or subservient to it in such a way that we are no longer troubled by the conflicting claims:

> usura
> blunteth the needle in the maid's hand
> and stoppeth the spinner's cunning.

But before we deal any further with canto 45, which gives us our first definite statement as to what a part, at least, of the poem is about, it will be better if we go back to the beginning of the *Decad*. The first two cantos deal with the founding of a 'damn good bank', the Monte dei Paschi, making clear an earlier reference on the second last page of canto 41 which to most readers must have been double Dutch. Cantos 42 and 43 are clear in outline if not always in detail, well written if sometimes rather long-winded, and contain only a few lines here and there of unfortunate foreign-matter, e.g. the opening lines of canto 42, the meaning of which is obscure even if we know what they are about. The ellipsis in canto 43 from the responsibility of the Sienese to the irresponsibility of the Sicilian racketeer is well done (as long, that is, as we consult chapter 3 of *Guide to Kulchur*) but there is still some doubt whether the lines beginning 'Out of Syracuse' and ending 'wouldn't swallow it' refer to a single episode or to two. The bare statement, 'more stew about the black money (lead money)' in canto 43 is unsatisfactory as communication. If it is not worth more space, why put it in? It means nothing in its present form and can only annoy. But the worst that can be said of these two cantos, taken as a whole, is that they go on too much about banking. 'All of this is important' he tells us, overloading us now with superfluous detail where before he refused us even a clue to the bare essentials. The best that can be said in their favour is that the style, as in the 'four fat oxen' passage, makes the reading worth while. The last few lines of canto 43, about the Florentine debt at the end of the Medici period, lead up to the reforms carried out in Tuscany shortly afterwards by Pietro Leopoldo and his son Ferdinando (cantos 44 and 50). Canto 44 is clear enough in outline, if we ignore some of the middle section, and towards the end clear in detail. In praising Pietro, 'who wished state debt brought to an end . . . who freed the printers of surveillance . . . who abolished death as a penalty and all tortures in prisons', Pound allows us for once to see exactly what he means and where he stands. From Pietro and Ferdinando we jump back rather disconcertingly by way of Napoleon's mother, to the Monte dei Paschi, with an official telling us that it—we take it that 'The foundation, Siena' refers to the bank—has served 'to keep bridle on usury'.

Canto 45, *With Usura*, is a statement, the clearest we get in the whole work, of Pound's 'position'. From it we learn something about his ideas of good and evil; we see what he is against and what he is for: the one against the other at close quarters, in unmistakeable opposition. And once we understand this opposition we are better placed to observe the import of a number of earlier passages and to appreciate more fully, even if we cannot share, his Eleusis. For although canto 45 cannot be said to rise naturally out of the preceding 230 pages, it reveals immediately the idealism at the root of his righteousness.

Pound does not accept, or himself formulate, a position in keeping with the reality of material and spiritual things. He dreams a beautiful dream, and interprets the outside world accordingly. Only that which can immediately be accommodated to the dream is real or good. Anything else is unreal or bad, or at any rate can safely be ignored. The contents of the poem, which earlier might have seemed to be broad and embracing, are now seen to be the filling-out of the dream with facts, to make it appear real. This does not mean that we are able to understand everything that has gone before. Only that a few points are clearer and that many passages and connexions still unexplained are now less likely to inhibit our determination to keep looking for the meaning of the work as a whole.

I have said that he dreams a dream, but it does not follow that the poet saw it in this light. He regarded the *Cantos* as firmly rooted in reality: a reality as broad and as deep as human history. What I have called a dream he saw as directly related to the Creator's design for the universe. And where I have spoken of him as ignoring the outside world, except in so far as it illustrates his point, he thought of the poem as in touch with, and rising out of, all essential facets of human life. Only once that I know of, in *Kulchur*, did he betray any doubt about the reality of his conception. But it was not until the *Pisan Cantos* that he altered his terminology and began to speak of his world as a dream. He does not seem to have appreciated the significance of this, and in *Rock-Drill* and *Thrones* went back to his earlier way.

The hard and fast opposition in canto 45, and again in 51, is between the natural and the unnatural. Between fecundity, natural increase, abundance, on the one hand, and artificial scarcities, on the other. And so it goes on, until we reach intuitively the idea of good religion as working hand in hand with God for the propagation of all good things, and bad religion as restrictive belief that works against this natural creativity. Two essays, one written in 1934, the other in 1942, may be taken as gloss on the text. Extracts will show what I mean. The first is from 'Date Line':

> By 1934 Frazer is sufficiently digested for us to know that opposing systems of European morality go back to the opposed temperaments of those who thought copulation was good for the crops, and the opposed faction who thought it was bad for the crops (the scarcity economists of pre-history). That ought to simplify a good deal of argument. The Christian might at least decide whether he is for Adonis or Atys, or whether he is Mediterranean. The exact use of dyeing Europe with a mythology elucubrated to explain the thoroughly undesirable climate of Arabia Petraea is in some reaches obscure.

The second is from the English version of *Carta da Visita*:

> The power of putrefaction aims at the obfuscation of history; it seeks to destroy not one but every religion, by destroying the symbols, by leading off into theoretical argument. Theological disputes take the place of contem-

plation. Disputation destroys faith, and interest in theology eventually goes out of fashion: not even theologians themselves take any more interest in it.

The power of putrefaction would destroy all intrinsic beauty. It is spread like the bacilli of typhus or bubonic plague, carried by rats wholly unconscious of their role.

Suspect anyone who destroys an image, or wants to suppress a page of history.

Latin is sacred, grain is sacred. Who destroyed the mystery of fecundity, bringing in the cult of sterility? Who set the Church against the Empire? Who destroyed the unity of the Catholic Church with this mud-wallow that serves Protestants in the place of contemplation? Who decided to destroy the mysteries within the Church so as to be able to destroy the Church itself by schism? Who has wiped the consciousness of the greatest mystery out of the mind of Europe, to arrive at an atheism proclaimed by Bolshevism?

Who has received honours by putting argumentation where before had been faith?

Who, what is more, attacks, continuously, the nerve centres, the centres of communication between nation and nation?

*　　*　　*

To replace the marble goddess on her pedestal at Terracina is worth more than any metaphysical argument.

And the mosaics in Santa Maria in Trastevere recall a wisdom lost by scholasticism, an understanding denied to Aquinas.

Let us see now what we can learn about the poem if we treat canto 45 as our starting-point. First, the opening words, 'With usura', and the ruin and decay which Pound attributes to this evil. Connexions come immediately to mind: Baldy Bacon whose interest 'Was in money business' (canto 12); the 'Hell' cantos, numbers 14 and 15, ('the beast with the hundred legs, USURA'); the First World War (16); Metevsky, etc. (18); economic sabotage in 19 ('And that invention, patent, is still in their desk') and intellectual sabotage in 22 ('I would like to accept C. H.'s book but it would make my own seem so out of date'); life under nineteenth-century industrialism (33); Central Europe (35); the American 'bank war' (37); the armaments industry (38); the waste of the tax system (41); and public debt (43 and 44).

The root is usury. Sometimes as the direct cause, but more often apparently the indirect, as when it creates a context for evil or the state of mind by which evil occurs. Pound himself might claim that usury as such is not the ultimate evil but only the tool of a certain type of mind. But this is not clear here. We must stick to what the poem says, or seems to say. If we begin interpreting too far away from the text, we shall become, as in fact some have, co-authors with Pound of a new work. And so it needs to be said that the ruin and decay laid at usury's door, if we take canto 45 as the pivot round which the rest revolves, are not always shown to be linked with it in any historical sense, nor do they appear always to be connected with it by any deep undertone poetically. The most we have to go on much of the time is the poet's superbly expressed conviction that this is the way the world is.

The positive side of canto 45 likewise points back to previous passages.

> wool does not come to market
> sheep bringeth no gain with usura

suggests the foundation of the Monte dei Paschi largely upon income derived from grazing ('there first was the fruit of nature') and the founders' emphasis upon the right use of its money:

> that the specie
> be lent to whomso can best use it USE IT
> (*id est, più utilmente*)
> to the good of their houses, to benefit of their business
> as of weaving, the wool trade, the silk trade . . .

As a highly condensed account of the good life, the canto seems to reach back to the line, 'Grass nowhere out of place', in 43, and forward to its appearance again in 51 and 74. Back also to

40: 'Towards producing that wide expanse of clean lawn', and to the achievement of Sigismundo and the Venetians recorded in the *Draft of XXX Cantos*. But the most significant thing in 45 is the introduction in this context of Eleusis:

> Usura slayeth the child in the womb
> It stayeth the young man's courting
> It hath brought palsey to bed, lyeth
> between the young bride and her bridegroom
> CONTRA NATURA
> They have brought whores for Eleusis

Putting together the evidence from a number of sources I would suggest that Pound regarded this as a Catholic idea. But the church of which it was the doctrine, consisted of two parts. The visible church called Catholic which is found in its pure state, we infer, only among certain Italians, and the hidden part, an underground order of initiates, going back to Eleusis. I am not clear about the exact relation between visible church and invisible; but it would seem that the visible is only to be regarded as the Catholic Church, in so far as it is permeated by traces of the Eleusinian mysteries. Here is a relevant passage from *Kulchur*:

> Great Intelligence attains again and again to great verity. The Duce and Kung fu Tseu equally perceive that their people need poetry; that prose is NOT education but the outer courts of the same. Beyond its doors are the mysteries. Eleusis. Things not to be spoken save in secret.
> The mysteries self-defended, the mysteries that *can* not be revealed. Fools can only profane them. The dull can neither penetrate the secretum nor divulge it to others.

*   *   *

> ... It is quite useless for me to refer to Provence, or to speculate on Erigena in the market place.

Detailed examination of the growth of this view is here out of the question. But if we allow it as a framework into which the 'Contra Natura' idea fits then the main stimuli towards the latter were I think two: Dante (particularly *Inferno* XV, XVI, and the meeting with the beast Geryon, XVII) and, strange to say, the following short passage from Joyce's *Portrait*:

—Then, said Cranly, you do not intend to become a protestant?
—I said that I had lost the faith, Stephen answered, but not that I had lost selfrespect. What kind of liberation would that be to forsake an absurdity which is logical and coherent and to embrace one which is illogical and incoherent?

I remember this came up seven years ago when I was editing a number of previously uncollected writings by Pound for publication by Regnery of Chicago under the title *Impact* (1960). Both Pound and I were living at the time at Schloss Brunnenburg, his daughter's home near Merano in Northern Italy. I remember asking him whether he wanted to alter, or tone down, a reference to Protestants. He said no, it should stay as it was, and quoted the Joyce, or something very like it, in defence. How early this passage, fortified perhaps by conversations with Joyce on the same theme, took root I do not know—Pound first saw a typescript of the *Portrait* in 1914—but he came to believe that Catholicism had retained certain powers lost by the Protestant world, including the power to sense 'mental and spiritual rottenness'.

The line, 'They have brought whores for Eleusis', would seem to mean that coition with a whore is our modern equivalent, in a world eaten by usury, of the ritual coition of Eleusis. This takes us back to the Provençal love ritual of canto 6 and the suggestion of an underground tradition in 36. It points also to canto 39, Odysseus' copulation with Circe, and the chant to Venus immediately after. Pound may also mean us to see a connexion between the lines:

with the Goddess' eyes to seaward
By Circeo, by Terracina, with the stone eyes
white toward the sea

(canto 39)

and the mention of Circeo again a few pages further on:

> Having drained off the muck by Vada
> From the marshes, by Circeo, where no one else wd. have
> > drained it.
> Waited 2000 years, ate grain from the marshes
> > (canto 41)

The first refers to his desire for the replacement of a statue of Venus on her pedestal at Terracina, the second to Mussolini's draining of swamp in the same area. Venus and fruitfulness thus linking up with the constructive ruler who turned the swamp into grainland.

I think it best if we leave this now without trying to push too far the claims of canto 45 to stand as pivot for the rest. We will take up the same threads again later.

Canto 46 we notice is divided more or less into two parts. In the first we see constructive men—Orage, Douglas and Mussolini—and hear reports on the Near East from Poundian 'live men' who have been there, seen for themselves and know what they are talking about. At least, this is how I interpret it. And in the second part we have a continuation of the 'Hell' cantos, a description of the world in which the constructive men labour. The opening is clear enough, down to 'get through hell in a hurry'. The nature description which follows is not obviously connected with the rest of the canto, which for our purposes would seem to begin again with:

> > Seventeen
> Years on this case, nineteen years, ninety years
> > on this case . . .

The canto was written about 1935. Seventeen years before would have been 1918, about the time Pound first met Douglas. The meaning then may be that the poet has spent seventeen years investigating economics. Nineteen years, 1916, might refer to the time he first began to get an inkling of this side of world affairs from those he met in Orage's office. Early in 1917, for example, he wrote in the article 'Anachronism at Chinon':

49

'no man is free who has not the modicum of an income'. He displays a similar concern with economics in part one of 'The Serious Artist' first published in the *New Freewoman* of 15 October 1913. The 'ninety years' possibly is meant to take us back to the earlier denunciations of the industrial system in canto 33. And the six lines that follow might be understood thus. Ezra Pound ('the fuzzy bloke') after listening to Douglas describe the shortcomings of the financial system, put forward the suggestion that if what Douglas said was true then 'any government worth a damn' could pay dividends to its citizens. 'The major' (Douglas), after thinking it over for a while, replied: You mean pay out dividends instead of collecting taxes? To which Pound answered: Yes, instead of collecting taxes. It was Pound, in other words, who forced Douglas to see that the consequences of his thinking was 'national dividends'. The following statement by Pound in 1957 would seem to place this interpretation beyond any reasonable doubt:

> Thought is not a personal possession. It often comes of collaboration. To the best of my memory, I said: 'In that case any government worth a damn could pay dividends instead of collecting taxes.' Just as it was Rossoni who said: E così lo stato fa il suo affare.
>
> This is not put down from vanity or for the sake of glory. There is no pretense to originality, as my remark was due to what C. H. D. had learned in India, vigorously stated by him on a particular day in the *New Age* office. Without his knowledge I should have remained ignorant . . .[1]

It is unlikely, however, that we would arrive at this interpretation on the strength of the canto alone. Outside knowledge is essential. As it is also for interpreting the next six lines. The words 'That office?', refer to the *New Age*. Those that follow, 'Didja see the Decennio?', to the exhibition held in 1932 to celebrate the tenth anniversary of Italian Fascism.

Orage's office, he is saying, was like the one from which Mussolini ran the newspaper *Il Popolo* about the same time. The

[1] *Edge*, No. 3, February 1957.

crime of two centuries, culminating in the First World War in
which five million were killed, refers I imagine to the founding
of the Bank of England in 1694. But it might on the other hand
mean simply that the war came about from two centuries of
European mismanagement. He then suggests that the American
Civil War was caused by debt rather than slavery, but leaves it
open and inserts a question-mark. When, immediately afterwards, Max Beerbohm is introduced:

> couple of Max's drawings,
> one of Balfour and a camel, an'
> one w'ich fer oBviOus reasons haz
> never been published, ole Johnny Bull with a 'ankerchief.
> It has never been published . . .

we are faced again with two defects which have troubled us
considerably already: Pound's habit of thinking we share his
thoughts, and the ineffectiveness of the 'repeats' and 'echoes'.
The drawing of Balfour I must leave to others more skilled in
research than I. The John Bull drawing however has already
been mentioned in canto 35:

> 'Victoria?
> 'Where 'ave I 'eard that nyme?'

How, I ask, could we possibly link this, without prior knowledge, to the drawing? And yet it is, according to Pound in
private conversation, the caption, and both, as far as I can see,
are meant to stand for the same thing. Even granting prior
knowledge there is no certainty we would connect them sixty-
five pages apart, or hold either, or both, in our heads until
canto 97:

> 'Victoria, Victoriaa, w'ere 'ave I 'eard that nyme?'

The line, 'trouble iz that you mean it, you never will be a
journalist', is Orage's opinion of Pound. And the thirty lines
which follow are probably the observations during tea at
Surbiton, Surrey, of Marmaduke Pickthall and the founder of
Bahai, on the differences between Europe and the Near East.

The first part particularly, about the camel driver, is difficult to follow unless we remember this from a letter by Pound to W. H. D. Rouse in 1937: 'Pickthall who knows his Near East, said veracity is only valued where people are in a hurry and set value on quickness.' Time and again we seem to be reading notes towards a poem rather than the finished work. If I continue in detail it is not because I think the canto is altogether worth it, either as poetry, history or anything else, but to explain a point regarded by Pound as central to his historical argument and to throw further light perhaps on the method. The statement on banking:

> Said Paterson:
>> Hath benefit of interest on all
> the moneys which it, the bank, creates out of nothing.

was taken I think from Christopher Hollis's *Two Nations*. William Paterson, identified by Pound only as 'Paterson', was a Scot who in the 1680s or thereabouts put forward a project which after one or two false starts became the Bank of England. The words quoted are from Paterson's prospectus. Although the Bank eventually succeeded, Paterson did not, and was later involved in the disastrous Darien expedition. Pound's Paterson in fact is not nearly as interesting as the historical one. But the point about the underlined words is that Pound is placing his finger on what he believes to be the crux. A strange way to do it, one might think, without either date or at least a few details, but that obviously is his intention. As far as he is concerned, he is, with that single quotation, laying bare the core of modern history. The statement he attributes immediately after to a member of the Rothschild family is meant as an extension of this:

> Semi-private inducement
> Said Mr. Rothschild, hell knows which Roth-schild
> 1861, '64 or there sometime, 'Very few people
> 'will understand this. Those who do will be occupied
> 'getting profits. The general public will probably not
> ' see it's against their interest.'

Very few people understand how the modern banking and funding system works; those who don't are harmless because they will not see that it is against their own interests; and the few who do will be no problem because they will be busy taking advantage of their know-how. A statement, more or less the same as the one given by Pound above in quotation marks, has been circulating among monetary reformers for many years, but I have never been able to discover definitely where it came from. Pound took it most likely from one of the American monetary reform papers of the 1930s or possibly Willis Overholser's pamphlet *Short Review and Analysis of the History of Money in the United States* (Libertyville, Illinois, 1936). In canto 46 the words are attributed to a Rothschild. But in all versions I have been able to locate they were written *to* the Rothschilds in London by or on behalf of an American politician John Sherman. The Rothschilds then repeated them, as coming from Sherman, in a letter dated 25 June 1863 to the New York bank of Ickleheimer, Morton and Van der Gould. There is no point in going further in explanation of this or the Paterson. For that would be to go beyond any meaning we can find in the poem. It is important to understand that Pound had not at this stage defined usury. He was not clear as to the extent to which interest on money created 'out of nothing' was usurious. But he could see (further on in the canto) that the purpose of this money was 'to meet a need'. This created for him a difficulty, which, even if he did not face it directly, or own it even to himself, is certainly present in the canto and the work as a whole. The exact relation, for example, between usury and the other parts of the poem is nowhere established. There are, in fact, large gaps in the text which are real and not just apparent. What holds the work together so far is simply Pound's going ahead and acting as if the connexions existed.

The assertion in canto 46 about Regius Professorships' being founded 'to spread lies and teach whiggery' is again from Hollis's *Two Nations*. Pound implies that it was the bankers, as usual, who from behind the scenes pulled the strings. Hollis's book is not, I suspect, very good history, even though it contains much that is true. It is, rather, propaganda, written at a time when men of good will were horrified by the failure or inability of the Capitalist system to alleviate the misery it had caused. But it should be noted that where Hollis restricts himself to a certain definite area, Pound's method, rather than Pound himself, makes the reference apply to almost anything having to do with lies or whiggery. Some have praised his use of others' material, without making a necessary distinction: you have, on the one hand, the acknowledged use of another's statement as such, in which case the user is bound to keep the author's intention in view. And on the other hand you have theft: the use of another's work for your own purposes. Legitimate, presumably, as long as you succeed in transforming it into your own and making it part of your own work. In which case, the original author is no longer responsible for it. There is also the ironic use of another's words for some purpose for which they were not intended. But this, let us be quite clear, depends on their original meaning, on your audience's knowing what they originally stood for. Otherwise there is no point.

But what Pound sometimes seems to be doing is trying to have a foot in both camps. He supports his own work with the authority of another, at the same time falsifying the statement and turning it to his own purpose. It is not that he intends outright to falsify. Rather he extends his authority's statement because he believes that it does indeed apply more widely, e.g. that what Christopher Hollis says about Regius Professorships may be linked with John Adams on the destruction of records (canto 33), and extended almost indefinitely. But with the result that specific lies become any lies you like to mention, and a history contained within certain limits becomes limitless. Pound does not say, I will show that what Hollis says about Regius Professors' falsifying history at a certain time and place is in fact true of many other periods, indeed of all history. Instead he wavers ambiguously between Hollis's history and his own wider view, drawing upon the former without accepting responsibility for the heavier load with which he burdens it, nor providing even for its maintenance and support. This imprecision, it is now beginning to appear, is the essence of Pound's method. What is supposed to be a mosaic, as it were, of the concrete and clear-edged, changes, under our very gaze, into a hodgepodge. The more we look, the less we find. The more we learn of his words, the less able are we to understand his meaning.

These ideas might be drawn out in detail and distinctions confirmed without helping us any further with the poem. The point we have established is that as soon as we begin to dig into the *Cantos* numerous problems of interpretation arise of a nature to arouse suspicion about its status as a controlled work of art.

The rest of canto 46, from 'The Macmillan Commission' to the end, is splendid rhetoric which carries the reader along even where there may be doubt about the meaning. We get the full flavour only if we know all the cantos well, plus half a dozen of Pound's prose works and a number of uncollected articles. Thus the lines:

Before that was tea dumped into harbour, before that was a
great deal still in the school books, placed there
NOT as evidence. Placed there to distract idle minds . . .

are easier to connect with Paterson and the Bank of England if we read these paragraphs from the English version of the 1944 pamphlet *L'America, Roosevelt e le cause della guerra presente*:

If you can understand the cause, or causes, of one war,
you will understand the cause or causes of several—perhaps
of all. But the fundamental causes of war have received
little publicity. School-books do not disclose the inner
workings of banks. The mystery of economics has been
more jealously guarded than were ever the mysteries of
Eleusis. And the Central Bank of Greece was at Delphi.
    . . . Regius professorships were founded to falsify history
and teach whiggery. And even the Tudor monarchs used
to talk about 'tuning the pulpits'.
    The cardinal fact of the American Revolution of 1776
was the suppression, in 1750, of the paper money issue in

Pennsylvania and other colonies, but history as taught in the U.S.A. speaks of more picturesque matters, such as the Boston Tea Party.

The lines:

> 'I rule the Earth' said Antoninus 'but LAW rules the sea'
> meaning, we take it, lex Rhodi, the law Maritime
> of sea lawyers.

need to be seen against this passage from 'The Individual in his Milieu' (1935):

> The archaeologist and serendipidist can wander back through Claudius Salmasius and find the known beginnings of usury entangled with those of marine insurance, sea lawyers, the law of Rhodes, the disputed text of Antoninus Pius on the limits of his jurisdiction.

and this (and the rest of chapter 3) from *Kulchur*:

> In 138 A.D. Antoninus Pius was considering the difference between Roman Law and the Law of Rhodes, between agrarian usury and maritime usury, he was concerned as to whether the Roman State shd. profit by sailor's misfortune and batten on shipwreck.

Some items in the canto, such as 'Brazilian coffee' and the building of St Peters, require a knowledge of numerous other works from which it would be fruitless to quote, except at much greater length than is here possible or even desirable. We will take up related aspects later with *Rock-Drill* and *Thrones*.

The remaining five cantos of the *Decad* underline, and perhaps develop, the points already made. Numbers 47, 49, and 51 continue to elaborate the idea of the natural against the unnatural, and to imply a mysterious relation between coition and intelligence. Cantos 48 and 50 continue with history and the good rulers. The overall purpose of 47 would seem to be clear, even if the details and construction are not. It begins with intelligence:

> Who even dead, yet hath his mind entire!

and the search for knowledge:

> Yet must thou sail after knowledge . . .

turns then to the death of Adonis, to be taken I suppose as a symbol of fertility:

> flower from the swift seed . . .

and moves then by way of woman ('To that is she bent'), natural magnetism ('Moth is called over mountain'), and man's place in the natural order ('Begin thy plowing . . .'), to coition and light:

> The light has entered the cave. Io! Io!
> The light has gone down into the cave,
> Splendour on splendour!
> By prong have I entered these hills . . .

Dione, the mother of Venus, is named in connexion with Adonis, instead of Venus herself, despite the fact that it was the daughter who loved Adonis and caused the anemone to spring up from his blood after he was killed by a boar. But this may be part of a mythological puzzle, which, solved, will aid us towards the meaning of the canto. Dante in canto 22 of the *Paradiso* uses the name *Maia* to mean her son Hermes, and Dione to mean her daughter Venus. Pound, in canto 47, says of Odysseus, a few lines after his reference to Dione, that 'By Molü art thou freed from the one bed that thou may'st return to another'. The drug moly was given to him by Hermes to counter the charms of Circe and enable him to return to Penelope. The death of Adonis then may stand for the male 'death' after copulation, which frees Odysseus from one kind of sexual encounter—sex as a drug or release—to pursue a higher—the ceremonial encounter of the Eleusinian mysteries. Be that as it may, the link between this canto and the Provençal love rite which is mentioned earlier is certain. The lines:

> Hast'ou a deeper planting, doth thy death year
> Bring swifter shoot?

and

That the grass grow from my body

take us back to canto 6:

> The stone is alive in my hand, the crops
> will be thick in my death-year . . .

Basically, Pound's attitude to life is simple and straightforward, and we ought always to remember this. 'A civil society', he says in *Kulchur*, 'is one where Strength comes with enjoyment. I am not trespassing into politics with this statement. A democracy run by clean men, decent men, honest men cd. or shd. attain Kraft durch Freude quite as well as a "dictatorship".' Also worth noting before we move on is the lapse of diction in 'So full of knowing that the beefy men know less than he', and the sometimes naïve movement recalling *Imagism* and earlier:

> The light has entered the cave. Io! Io!
> The light has gone down into the cave,
> Splendour on splendour!

We shall not stop at canto 48, except to note the obscurity. What, for example, has the puppy's pedigree got to do with the other private letter (' "while she bought 2 prs of shoes" '), or the private letter with interest rates in Bithynia or the beautifully evoked Provençal landscape? Who could disentangle the lines about the ant and the ox-carcase, even knowing the relevant passage in *Jefferson and/or Mussolini*? And the last five lines seem almost wilfully obscure. The old man was employed to place a stone on the long beach costumes, to stop them from billowing in the wind. Instead of saying that, Pound cuts away the substance and leaves us with a puzzle.

Canto 49 we can afford to skip. Its beauty is beyond question, its place clear in the poet's vision of a well-ordered natural world. Canto 50 continues an historical vein already met with. We shall have occasion to return to it when discussing some of the later cantos. Considered in the round canto 51 falls into the same category as 45. But a few details will bear comment. The line, 'Fifth element; mud; said Napoleon', squeezed between God shining in the mind of heaven and the anti-usury chant, has been described as a tribute to Napoleon's fight against usury. This may be its purpose. It would be difficult to argue convincingly otherwise, since we have so little to go on. In favour of this interpretation is the fact that Pound at this stage was reading R. McNair Wilson, who was convinced that Napoleon's struggle was directed against the 'money power'. Either way, however, the method stands condemned. It allows you to say everything without committing yourself to anything. Conceived in the interests of clarity, or so we believe, it ends in pretentious unmeaningness, with the poet sheltering behind a 'system' of unresolved implications: words, phrases, lines and passages placed together in such a way that they imply the possibility of a meaning that is not actually there. The reader is all the time being encouraged to think that there is a design behind the apparent haphazardness, when in fact any enquiry and construction relating and comparing any two or more of the points made by Pound, will in most cases take him far beyond the limits of the poet's knowledge. After the anti-usury chant is a long passage on fly-fishing, which is meant, I take it, to illustrate man's working in conjunction with nature, his participation, almost, in the forms he helps to create, an interpretation strengthened by the lines which follow and the quotation from Albertus about the power of the intellect. The 'Konigsberg' interlude says that two peoples have achieved a *modus vivendi*. But what peoples, who said it, or why, we are not told. Its meaning may be that nations, too, have a place in the natural order, but that is only guesswork. The Chinese sign at the end of the canto has for Pound a meaning that is well rendered in English by Newman's 'call things by their right names'.

Repetitions inside the *Decad*, in addition to those already mentioned, include: Antoninus (cantos 42 and 46); 'ob pecuniae scarcitatem' (42 and 43); debt under the Medici (43 and 50); and 'the power over wild beasts' (47 and 49). Whatever their purpose, they contribute only vaguely as reminders, and not at all as structure. Any more than do the following links between the *Fifth Decad* and earlier cantos: 'Thou shalt not always walk in the sun' (42) and Tovarisch (27); Regius Professorships, etc. (46), Van Buren's Autobiography 'put in the cellarage' (48) and Adams's statement on the destruction of records (33); 'helandros kai heleptolis' (46) and Eleanor 'destroyer of cities' (2, etc.); Tiresias (47, 39, 2 and 1); 'become fathers of the next generation' (48 and 33); 'spire-top a-level the grass yard' (48 and 29); 'the power over wild beasts' (49, 47 and 2); ' "Revolution" said Mr. Adams' (50 and 32); 'Fifth element; mud' (51 and 34); and 'hath the light of the doer' (51 and 25). Many items found in the *Fifth Decad*, and earlier, appear again later. Regius Professorships, echoed several times in the China and Adams cantos, turn up again in canto 86, there commenting on the history of ancient Greece and still more ancient Babylon.

I may perhaps express our general view by saying that the *Fifth Decad* is decisive. We see now something of what Pound is trying to do. At the same time we feel compelled to decide that the work is not what it is supposed to be. The final lines on 'Hell', are excellent; 'oily wind' and 'sour song' are Pound at his best. But like so many others in the *Cantos*, belong to a poem that has never been written.

V

CHINA AND ADAMS 1940

IT IS SOMETIMES HELD that the John Adams section (cantos 62-71) is closely related to the preceding section on China (52-61). The argument in favour of this view, put most simply, is as follows. The eighty pages of Chinese history demonstrate how things run smoothly when rulers and people obey the Confucian 'law', and fall apart when they neglect it. The eighty pages on John Adams depict a wise, Confucian-type ruler in action in the American colonies and early United States. Have we any reason to believe that this is not a fair interpretation of these twenty cantos? The answer, if we look at them carefully, is in the affirmative: there is plenty of reason.

I would observe, firstly, that an assertion or denial of the connexion between China and Adams can hardly be proved, in any strict sense, unless we go into the matter much more fully than Pound has. And secondly, even if it could be proved historically or philosophically, which Pound does not begin to do, either in the *Cantos* or elsewhere in his writings, there is still the (to us, more important) question of poetry: is the connexion conveyed poetically? Here we are forced to say definitely not. There is, to begin with, none of that acute psychological understanding which is one of the first and most obvious marks of a poetic intelligence at work upon, interpreting and drawing together, hidden threads in the world about. Nor anything special about the language which might lead us to suppose that the poet is reading between the lines, recording fine points, and making

61

sense out of the flux. Nothing, in other words, to inspire confidence, and much, as I shall show, to shake it.

It is advisable to say something here about the conditions under which these cantos were written. Most of them would seem to date from the latter half of 1937 to the first half of 1939. Pound gives 'January 1938' as the date (of the first draft, presumably) of canto 62. In a letter dated May 1938 he says he is reading Moyriac de Mailla's *Histoire Générale de la Chine* (Paris, 1777-85), which is the source of the China cantos, and speaks in another, dated February 1939, of the Adams cantos as being in 'rough typescript'. A look at his contributions to periodicals at this time is revealing. Out of eighty items published between January 1938 and July 1939, twenty-three were for Sir Oswald Mosley's *Action* or *British Union Quarterly*, and a dozen for Mairet's *New English Weekly*. Forty more items, at least, published in other journals, were distinctly political or ideological in flavour. Pound's association with the Mosley organization was more than incidental. In March and April 1938 he helped A. Raven Thomson, a Mosley official, to revise his pamphlet *The Coming Corporate State*, and a month or so later Thomson edited and rearranged the original text of Pound's *What is money for?* for publication early the following year by Mosley's Greater Britain Publications. Not that Pound supported Mosley exclusively, or in one sense at all. For he was not really interested in the British Union Movement, nor any other of the numerous movements with which he was in touch, except in so far as they might forward his own monetary and racial-religious ideas. He was capable also of supporting a movement simply because it was active. What it was active about didn't always seem to matter a great deal to him, so long as it was moving. He felt, I suppose, that one had a better chance of doing something useful with a movement once it was on the march.

It would be a mistake to place too much reliance on this aspect of his work as a guide to the *Cantos*. The Adams section, written shortly before his 1939 trip to the United States, during which he tried to interest politicians and others in his ideas for keeping the peace between Italy and the U.S., would seem to be free of these immediate influences; certainly, is not aimed or diluted so as to accord with them. But the same cannot be said for the China cantos. They manifest a decided decline in mental awareness and use of language, a gullibility, if I may so term it, in the face of political catch-phrases, which might well be the result of an exhausting involvement in current affairs. While we cannot, I feel sure, prove this, what we can do is to demonstrate the deterioration of language. This, after all, is the important thing, our interest in causes being purely secondary.

Broadly, the main defect may be summarized as an uncritical awe in the presence of things Chinese, which leads, firstly, to uncritical acceptance of what Pound believes to be a Confucian view of history, and thence to uncritical use of language. He is serious and approving when he says that in a certain age the schoolrooms in China had 'mottoes writ all over walls'. There is no qualification, no explanation, when we are told of a certain ruler that he 'dressed as one of the people' and cared 'for needs of the people'. A prince is described as 'friend of peace, friend of the people'. A journey is made 'for good of the state'. Once a year, in one reign, there was 'to the most honest citizens: a dinner at expense of the emperor', and 'woikinmen' who did their work according to the rules earned an '8th degree button and right to sit at tea with the governor'. Fascism ('rods in a bundle' and 'Ammassi') and Hitler ('Schicksal') are introduced for good measure. A little spark, we are told, 'lights a great deal of straw', and 'Kung is to China as is water to fishes'. There is endless 'tough-guy' talk which contrives unsuccessfully to convey more meaning than it is able to bear. Thus, 'Ouei prince went pussyfoot', 'The highbrows are full of themselves', 'fool litterati', and 'no slouch ever founded a dynasty'. While 'decent rulers' concentrate on 'internal order', the 'Swine think of extending borders'. Once or twice he introduces a note from *Cathay* ('He heard the wild goose crying sorrow' and 'sieges from the beginning of time until now'), and there are the usual fine passages:

And KAO went to Kung fu tseu's tomb out of policy
videlicit to please the writers and scholars
A hot lord and unlettered, that knew to correct his
own faults . . .

But there is far too much imprecise language, inferior thinking
and misplaced diction, for us to to be able to read for long with
undiluted pleasure.

We must not, however, neglect the fact that these twenty
cantos contain references to some of Pound's main economic
ideas and continue to develop earlier themes. Canto 52 continues the contrast stated in the *Fifth Decad*. We hear of the true
base of credit ('the abundance of nature with the whole folk
behind it'), and of Eleusis and Confucius. And waging war
against the natural scheme of things is usury and hyper-usury.
This latter Pound calls 'super-neschek', using the Hebrew word.
Super-neschek may be any usury on money created out of nothing,
usury on an international scale, or perhaps both. Pound is not
clear on this point, but the result is governments 'full of their
gun-swine, bankbuzzards, poppinjays'. The reference on the
second page of the canto to 'Gregory damned' is not, I think, to
the economist Guggenheim-Gregory, as some have suggested,
but to Pope Gregory and Gregorian chant, if we go by the
context and what Pound has written in canto 96 and elsewhere.

Of the fifteen or so references to money in the China cantos,
only three perhaps concern us immediately, the rest are better
treated on one side, for other reasons, later. The three are: the
making of copper money by 'Tching Tang', the first appearance
in the *Cantos* of one of Pound's favourite monetary nuggets, the
Greek *Metathemenon te ton krumenon*, from Aristotle's *Politics*, both
of these in canto 53, and the basis or germ, in canto 55, of the
idea, 'a share, not a fixed charge', in respect of taxation. All
three are to be met with again in later cantos.

The first, the making of copper money in time of drought,
so that the people might buy grain where grain was available,
represents the 'distributive' function of money. The 'Metathemenon' quotation means 'if those who use a currency give it

up in favour of another'. It is for Pound a means of underlining references to those who alter the value of a currency for gain.

In canto 53 it is 'King Wang' who 'thought to vary the currency ... and to gain by this wangling'. 'Ngan' in contrast (canto 55) fixed 'the value of money.' The third point, that a ruler should take a share of the nation's produce, rather than a fixed amount, crops up several times in canto 55 and again in the *Pisan Cantos, Rock-Drill* and *Thrones*. The idea, I think, is that if the ruler demands a fixed amount of rice per year— three hundred tons, say—this may be bearable in a good year but unbearable in a poor year or drought. If, however, he takes a share, his actual tonnage will go up or down according to the size of the crop. And so he lives in rhythm with his people and nature.

Given a knowledge of Pound's other writings, most readers could be expected to arrive at similar interpretation of these three points, which deserve serious consideration. We cannot, however, say the same of most of the other monetary references, in which we find the poet indulging in imprecision as a means, it would appear, of disguising, even from himself perhaps, the extent of his ignorance. In Canto 53: 'money was in days of Hoang Ti'. This is meaningless without knowledge of the kind of 'money', and there can be no knowledge of the kind without the historical context, neither of which is given. Canto 55: 'Chou coin was of iron, like Sparta's.' This sort of thing belongs to a past age of 'comparative' history and anthropology. The fact that many books and articles still reflect this age and method make no difference. Such comparison has no meaning unless we know precisely each money in its own immediate context and this means, further, in relation to its own historical background. We have in the same canto: 'Money and all that, stabilization, probably racket' (plus the date 1069, a play perhaps on *1066 and all that*). The inadequacy is self-evident, as it is in: 'Flood relief, due to Ngan? joker somewhere?' This is one of his less pleasing attitudes, the 'wise guy' who sees through the smokescreen, but takes care to paper over the gaps with imprecision, a 'probably', and a question-mark.

This brings us to a question of history, as well disposed of here as later. If we take Pound seriously, it may be argued, we must take seriously his history, even if only to show sometimes how bad it is. But this presupposes a set of conditions which does not exist. Presupposes an Ezra Pound whose serious probings deserve serious attention; and much more beside. The enquiring amateur is seldom aware of his arrogance. He does not see that a question can be as ignorant or as learned almost as an answer. A question—how often have we ourselves been guilty? —which demands a certain answer or a certain type of answer, or takes too much for granted, is not really a question at all. This is just as true when the presuppositions are unconscious. A good question requires care, in proportion, we might say, to our ignorance. And the almost silent revolution in historical studies over the past half-century, the immense amount of detailed work which has produced so many new facts, but no method of dealing with them, necessitates considerable delving even to discover a rough idea of the state of our own ignorance. It is bad enough when we demand of the professional an up-to-date answer to an out-of-date question. But to take Pound seriously as an historian, to look up his sources, discuss them, and so forth, is tantamount to giving nineteenth-century answers to a nineteenth-century question. This is justified when it is a case of exploring his own meaning, but we must not confuse it with history. It would be different if Pound had shown himself a scholar. We would owe him detailed attention. But it is not owed unless earned by systematic exploration properly articulated.

It may so happen that the amateur arrives at an historical truth—I mean a complex, not just a single fact—in advance of the historian. If he does, it is either by intuition, a reaching out to the facts without knowing them, or by lucky guess. But let us be clear what this means. The truth is not finally accepted as truth until scholars have discovered, tested and approved as genuine, a whole new series of additional facts. We do not know that it is the truth until the work has been done; up till then it is still a theory or a guess. It is not known to be true, no matter how right it is, until the relevant facts, discovered, assembled and interpreted, are brought into relation with the body of past knowledge.

If I have laboured the point it is because unrecognized it is the source of so much confusion. Not that I have fully defined it here—it would require a great deal more than I am able to contribute—but at least let us have fewer ill-advised statements about poets arriving at the truth by intuition. I do not deny poetic intuition, I should wish to defend it. But we have a right, a duty even, to demand, before defending it, that it is indeed that and not something else.

The China cantos exhibit few signs of such intuition and are not very useful as history, except perhaps if we want to get an idea of the sequence of dynasties, in which case it is much quicker to look at Appendix D of the *Annotated Index*. Pound's eighteenth-century source, de Mailla's *Histoire Générale*, is a great work which holds an important place in the annals of western awareness of China. But, through de Mailla's fault, or his own, Pound's cantos do not even begin to register the feel of Chinese history—the rise and fall, the depths, the long periods of chaos, or the extent of monetary depreciation and counterfeiting. But we ought to be grateful, even so, for passages that outlast the history. Also for the fact that in giving what he imagined to be an account of events and motives he was driven to formulate the monetary perceptions examined earlier.

The Adams section is one of the most forbidding, on the face of it, but successful, in the whole work. It lacks the poetic force of the *Pisan Cantos*, and the depth, but is in some respects better knit, more of a piece. It is a 'portrait' of John Adams in action in the flux of events. There is never any doubt where we are, or what we are doing, even when we may be ignorant of what Adams is talking about or the situation in which he is involved. Admittedly, it is at first sight the section most in need of reference-books. Names, dates, events, half-sentences and pronouncements out of context: we feel the need immediately to reach for *The Works of John Adams* (Boston, 1852-65), from which the substance is taken. But once we get into the swing of it we see that research adds little or nothing and may even obscure from us the direction. There is no doubt about Pound's being able to carry off the monetary points with style:

> Every bank of discount is downright corruption
> taxing the public for private individuals' gain.
>   and if I say this in my will
> the American people wd/ pronounce I died crazy.

And when he does find the right way to register an effect, the freshness is delightful:

> Routledge was elegant
> 'said nothing not hackneyed six months before'

and

> 'forward young man' wrote the critic
>   on an unsigned J. A. (J. A. being then 53 and
>   vice president)

The main fault of the section is that it is much too long. Another is that Pound mixes two methods, which is always dangerous. One moment he uses straight reporting, the next a system of artificial chops and changes. A pity that here, where the chop-and-change method is for the first and only time in the work successful for pages at a time, he should hesitate to take full advantage of it. The reason why it works here and seldom elsewhere is that for once he has a single point to stick to—John Adams—and does so. If it is not completely successful, and often tedious, it is because he cannot make up his mind whether he wants to give us a portrait of Adams at work or a history of 'what happened'.

The other faults of the Adams cantos are those already met with in the China section, that is, loose language masquerading as down-to-earth precision (canto 64: 'Re which things was Hutchinson undoubtedly scrofulous') and 'tough guy' talk which intrudes without warrant into the surrounding tone (canto 65: 'J. A. was out with a musket like any damn com-

68

mon marine'). Sometimes in his zeal for monetary reform he may be inclined to misread Adams's mood or tone. Not that Adams's ideas on money are likely to meet with approval exactly from a present-day banker, or be welcomed altogether by Americans of conservative tendency for whom he is one of their greatest thinkers. But neither are they, on the other hand, quite the same as the modern monetary reformer's. They may sometimes look the same in the abstract, but there is, I believe, a difference of attitude which makes all the difference in the end. Pound is conscious of Adams's refusal to get het up unnecessarily about things he was powerless to alter, and this knowledge is embodied in his handling of the other's writings. But it is possible he does not allow sufficiently for Adams's irony or see quite the extent to which Adams was prepared to suffer certain evils as ineradicable or less dangerous than any possible remedy.

Of connexions with other parts of the work I have said little because they do not, unless I misjudge them completely, add either to the twenty cantos under consideration or to our understanding of the rest. I do not find it illuminating that the opening lines of canto 52, easy and flowing in themselves, repeat the 'there first was the fruit of nature etc.' of canto 43. Or that the Chinese sign at the end of canto 52 in the New York edition (*chih*[3], 'to desist'), turns up again twice in canto 85, twice in 87, and once in 93. Nothing is gained from knowing that the phrase, 'ob pecuniae scarsitatem', first mentioned in 42, occurs again in 43 and 64. Examination of any of the following 'repeats' will confirm our estimate. First those within the section: 'Ammassi' or pooling system (cantos 53, 56, and 61); 'And they used paper notes,' (53 and 54); 'Schicksal' (56 and 62); Lord Coke (62, 63, 64 and 66); 'depreciation of money a tax' (68 and 69); and 'our trouble is iggurance of money' (70 and 71). 'Repeats' which link up with earlier sections include: 'Taught and the not taught' (63, 52, 51, 45 and 36); Confucius (69, 57, 56, 53, 52 and 13); 'Reason from heaven etc.' (65 and 51); Kublai (66 and 18); 'Kang Hi' (69 and 49); and Antoninus (61, 46 and 42). John Adams is mentioned in at least the following: 31, 32,

33, 48, 50, 52 and 62-71. Frobenius, first mentioned in 38, is referred to indirectly ('der im Baluba') in 53. We may also be meant to see a connexion between the Cadmus story in 27 and the five dead Americans of 62. And there is a thread perhaps joining the men 'who had lied for hire' in 14, the pamphleteers at 'a guinea a day' in 62, and those who 'will print anything that will sell' in 71. The 'dove sta memora' of 63 and 'formato loco' of 70 are from the *canzone* by Cavalcanti of which canto 36 is a translation. Two statements in 71, 'Histories are annihilated' and 'Civic polity ecclesiastical bigotry destroy everything etc.', refer back to the opening of 33, further echoes of which are found also in 46 ('Regius Professorships' and 'placed there to distract idle minds') and 48 (' "deface and obliterate" '). This idea of the corruption of history has many other echoes and possible echoes throughout, and may fairly be described as one of Pound's guiding ideas. By canto 94 the corruption is ascribed more or less directly to bankers or those behind them.

I have thought over whether to list the many Chinese signs and repetitions, and decided against it. I cannot see that they are of any real importance and after a time the hunt becomes farcical. Like all but a few readers of the poem I am totally ignorant of the written language of Ancient China. At one stage during my reading of Pound I sought some acquaintance with the subject. I soon discovered that what one scholar translated as 'dividing a field with justice' another said point-blank meant 'God distributes things'. Obviously one had to take up the subject, or retire, and I chose the latter. Two examples of Pound's method will suffice, after which the reader who disagrees about the importance of Chinese in the poem may pursue his own researches via the *Annotated Index* and a Chinese Dictionary.

The signs for 'call things by their right names' (*cheng*[4] *ming*[2]), placed at the end of canto 51, are repeated in English in 52 and given again in Chinese in 60, 63 (only the *cheng*[4]), 66, 67 (only the *cheng*[4]), 68 and again in 97. In all but the first case they seem only to reinforce surrounding references to accuracy of word. The 'Make It New' signs (*hsin*[1] *jih*[4] *hsin*[1]), first used in 54, are repeated in various ways in 54, 87, 93, 94, 96(?) and 98. Usually they underline ideas or hints of renewal or rebirth. Elsewhere, especially in *Rock-Drill* and *Thrones*, the method is not nearly as easy to follow and one would have to be a sinologist to discover what it is all about.

VI

THE PISAN CANTOS 1948

IN AN UNPUBLISHED LETTER to a friend more than fifty years
ago, Ezra Pound included on a separate sheet, dated 'Saturday',
the words, 'To build a dream over the world'. We have here the
germ of the *Pisan Cantos*. The 'Make strong old dreams' of *A
Lume Spento* and the 'dream' of the other early poems, in this line
isolated thus are brought to a new focus. Let us follow its
development. There is, first of all, talk in his correspondence
of the time, of reviving old pagan customs, of keeping a lamp
burning before a shrine. Complementary attitudes may be
discerned in the published work, poetry and prose, right through
until 1920. In cantos 4 and 5, published in 1919 and 1921, he
mentions Ecbatan, 'City of patterned streets', where the god
descended on Danäe in a golden shower. In 1920 or 1921 Pound
and the friend of the early letter together visited Brancusi's studio
in Paris and watched the sculptor at work on a column. These
facts, ideas and symbols—the dream, the shrine, the column,
the 'City of patterned streets'—began to merge and take new
shape in the poet's mind. By 1938 he is writing to the same
friend that 'after twenty years waiting' Brancusi is now building
the temple in India, and that the column 'of which you saw
the small start' is now set up at Jargu in Roumania. Two years
later he inserted in his own hand in a copy of *Cantos LII-
LXXI*, near the date 11 February 1940, the words:

> To build up the city of Dioce
> (Tan Wu Tsze)
> Whose terraces are the colour of stars

The Pisan Cantos 1948

Finally, in the *Pisan Cantos*, it became

> To build the city of Dioce whose terraces are
> the colour of stars.

But it is not just the single line we see developing, it is the whole section. The *Pisan Cantos* were made from the dreams that remained after his world had been destroyed in the Second World War. Viewed in this light they introduce us to the heart of his successes and failures as a poet. For it was only after he had been thrown into an American detention camp at Pisa, the political world in which he had placed so much trust in ruins around him, that he wrote his best poetry: not about history, economics, or the contemporary world, but woven out of dreams. Forced by circumstances to be true to his gift, he left the world of fact, as it is portrayed in the first seventy cantos, and gave himself over to another dimension, to register for the first time at length that aspect of being for which he had aptitude. Compare the heaviness of:

> The Prince of Ho-kien preferred histories, *Chu King*
> and the *Tcheou-li* and the *Li-ki* of Mencius (Mong-tsé)
> and the *Chi-king* or Odes of Mao-chi and the *Tchun-tsiou*
> with the comment of Tso-kieou-min.
> and the Li-yo with treatise on music.
>
> (canto 54)

with this from the *Pisan* section:

> that Ho-Kien heard the old Dynasty's music
> as it might be at the Peach-blossom Fountain
> where are smooth lawns with the clear stream
> between them, silver, dividing . . .
>
> (canto 84)

The reason for his long confusion and delay before this, is not far to seek. Pound inherited, naturally enough, the metaphysical poverty of the nineteenth century. We must notice two main features: the age's horror at the reality pressing in on it, and the way it dealt with the situation. It had no true metaphysics through which it might place in perspective the advances in

73

science and industry; and so, lost faith in a spiritual or meta-physical order beyond sensible nature. Fitzgerald's letter to Cowell (1847) is a pathetic admission of this:

> Yet, I often think, it is not the poetical imagination, but bare Science that every day more and more unrolls a greater Epic than the Iliad; the history of the World, the infini-tudes of Space and Time! I never take up a book of Geology or Astronomy but this strikes me. And when we think that Man must go on to discover in the same plod-ding way, one fancies that the Poet of today may as well fold his hands, or turn them to dig or delve, considering how soon the march of discovery will distance all his imagin-ations, and dissolve the language in which they are uttered ... So that, as Lyell says, the Geologist looking at Niagara forgets even the roar of its waters in the contemplation of the awful processes of time that it suggests. It is not only that this vision of Time must wither the Poet's hope of immortality, but it is in itself more wonderful than all the conceptions of Dante and Milton.

Those who did not go over to materialism, had not the equip-ment to deal with it. This is not the place to discuss, even if I were capable, the religious history of the time. Or describe, even briefly, the yearning reflection of a few of the more sensitive souls in a twilight world of doubt. The point is that they had no way of seeing that the spiritual order, approached first through the senses, is not exhausted by the sensible realities in which the intellect first discovers it. No way of grasping that metaphysical wisdom opens upon a world of realities which can exist apart from matter. Matter, which, ontologically speaking, is always in move towards unintelligibility. For in so far as things are 'immersed' in matter, just so far are they removed from pure intelligibility. In ignorance of such principles, the nineteenth century tried to face, and then either surrendered to, or turned away from, science and industrialism.

The result, for poetry, was a new encounter with dream and make-believe. Reality, science seemed to be saying, is composed entirely of matter. In which case, he, the poet, would turn away from reality and create worlds of his own, owing as little as possible to matter or the here and now. The weaknesses of nineteenth-century poetry have often been rehearsed. But loss of this kind in literature is seldom dead loss unaccompanied by compensation or gain. Sometimes, the very weaknesses of the century, the dream and regret, brought into contact with reality at the right moment, yield a note never before heard in English.

This then, roughly, was Pound's immediate heritage. He struggled to free himself but had not the means or ability to do so, except in respect of diction and technique. His intellectual struggle for more than thirty years was to escape from the dream atmosphere of nineteenth-century poetry into the world of reality and matter from which his predecessors had turned in fear, despair, or disgust. He wanted to escape the one and embrace the other, because, burdened by an inferior metaphysics, he feared that the world of matter was, if not the whole, then the main or most important portion of reality and in danger of passing him by. His concern with facts, his mixing in politics and economics, his insistence on 'scientific' precision in writing and 'scientific' method in criticism, was because he believed or suspected that *there* was the real world.

It is my intention to describe something of Pound's attitude to Italy and Germany, and state of mind during the war, in a biography now in preparation. It will serve our present purpose if I say only that his conduct between 1940 and 1945 makes a strange and fascinating story, as may be gathered from the following brief example. About 1944 he had printed on green paper at Rapallo a number of small posters, apparently for distribution or posting on walls, although I have no evidence that this actually occurred. Already in a pamphlet published in Italy in December 1942 he had explained that the most useful service he could do would be to place before the public every year a few lines from Confucius. This he now proceeded to follow out by having printed on strips twenty inches long such maxims (in Italian) as: 'The archer who misses the bulls-eye turns and seeks the cause of his failure in himself' and 'The unmixed functions without end, in time and space without end'. Fragments of the latter occur in canto 74 ('funge la purezza'), canto 80 ('senza termine funge'), and canto 85 ('che funge'). Another poster carried a message from Cavalcanti: 'Fashions a new person from desire.' It was time for a last-ditch stand: Confucius and Cavalcanti would be the rallying-points.

Within a short time the war was over, his worldly hopes shattered beyond repair. He was imprisoned by the Americans at Pisa. In the *Pisan Cantos* he leaves the world of facts, history and economics, and returns, fortified now by a mature technique, to the dream world of his early years. Fascism was dead, the Salò republic with which he had been associated finished. One of the themes of the Pisan section is decline and fall, decay and destruction, in the material world. All that really matters, he says, is the thing held in the mind. This aspect derives much from 'The legend of Gassire's lute', an African tale which Pound had from Frobenius:

Four times Wagadu stood there in all her splendour, four times Wagadu disappeared and was lost to human sight: once through vanity, once through falsehood, once through greed, and once through dissension. Four times Wagadu changed her name. First she was called Dierra, then Agada, then Ganna, then Silla. Four times she turned her face. Once to the north, once to the west, once to the east, and once to the south. For Wagadu, whenever men have seen her, has always had four gates: one to the north one to the west, one to the east, and one to the south. These are the directions whence the strength of Wagadu comes, the strength in which she endures no matter whether she be built of stone, wood, or earth, or lives but as a shadow in the mind and longing of her children. For really, Wagadu is not of stone, not of wood, not of earth. Wagadu is the strength which lives in the hearts of men and is sometimes visible because eyes see her and ears hear the clash of swords and ring of shields, and is sometimes invisible because the indomitability of men has overtired her, so that she sleeps. Sleep came to Wagadu for the first time through vanity, for the second time through falsehood, for the third time through greed, and for the fourth time through dissension. Should Wagadu ever be found for the fifth time, then she will live so forcefully in the minds of men that she will never be lost again, so forcefully that vanity, falsehood, greed and dissension will never be able to harm her. Hoooh! Dierra, Agada, Ganna, Silla! Hooh! Fasa!

Every time that the guilt of men caused Wagadu to disappear she won a new beauty which made the splendour of her appearance still more glorious. Vanity brought the song of the bards which all peoples (of the Sudan) imitate and value today. Falsehood brought a rain of gold and pearls. Greed brought writing as the Burdama practise it today, and which in Wagadu was the business of the women. Dissension will enable the fifth Wagadu to be as enduring as the rain of the south and as the rocks of the Sahara, for every man will then have the Wagadu in his heart and every woman a Wagadu in her womb. Hoooh! Dierra, Agada, Ganna, Silla! Hooh! Fasa![1]

'Four times,' Pound says in canto 74, 'was the city rebuilded.' This is the city of Dioce, as well as Wagadu, 'now in the mind indestructible'. Again and again the theme is taken up and repeated or rephrased:

> nothing matters but the quality
> of the affection—
> in the end—that has carved the trace in the mind
> dove sta memoria
> > (canto 76)

> 4 times was the city remade,
> now in the heart indestructible
> > (canto 77)

> to dream the Republic
> > (canto 78)

> What thou lov'st well shall not be reft from thee
> > (canto 81)

Pound struggles of course to retain the world of the earlier cantos. But if the facts are the same, the effect is different. In

[1] Leo Frobenius and Douglas C. Fox, *African Genesis*, London 1938.

canto 74, he refuses, for example, to surrender the American Constitution, meaning his own interpretation of it, which includes special emphasis on the section dealing with coinage. But his refusal to surrender fits neatly into the dream context:

> I surrender neither the empire nor the temples
> plural
> nor the constitution nor yet the city of Dioce . . .

The Pisan section would not be the success it is, if he had omitted all reference to fact, government, money and the here and now. What makes all the difference is the way he uses them. After years of writing on these subjects it was inevitable that certain aspects should have become part of his mind. And it is precisely as things held 'in the mind indestructible' that they are remembered and worked into these cantos. The Constitution here mentioned is not the document known to generations of American lawmakers and lawyers, the Mussolini of these cantos is not the man who really existed, they belong, rather, to the realm of what might have been. And so, dreams, experiences and perceptions, are woven together with the what-might-have-been of history and his interpretation of real events, to form a new unity. This unity is so remarkable, considering the jumble of materials out of which it is composed, that I feel compelled to notice it at some length. Two things, which by their absence from other sections lead to confusion, here by their presence mean success. They are unity of tone and logic of imagination.

The unity of tone is of a man remembering. The logic of imagination, while not altogether separate, reaches deeper. It can, and often does, in poetry, provide cohesion at a level too deep to plumb. Just so here. Sometimes, even where the surface connexion between images or ideas is bordering on the banal, a deeper 'logic' hidden but no less real holds them together. The poet, as unaware as we are, of what he is doing, or more so perhaps, is nevertheless touching something we all can feel.

Good imagery, we notice, does not operate through mere imagery alone, or any comparison we may draw between one thing and another. It draws on fantasy and abstract ideas

78

as well. The image, so called, is often made up of a single image, or one or more shifting images, which we can see, as if thrown onto a screen, plus some degree of comparison or metaphor, and, blended in with these, one or more abstract ideas. And each note, moreover, may have its own distinctive overtones. Impatience, quite justified, with bad imagery and undigested abstract statement, has caused us to overlook the important part which abstraction plays in good imagery. Most discussion goes astray in assuming that imagery exists only in the form of images we can see, as with the eye. But in fact the mind can see in various ways and at different levels. Whether the levels in imagery are unified, ignored, left separate, or only intermittently drawn together, depends on the education in poetry of the reader and the quality of the poem. But the point is that the mind can see things without necessarily forming a representational image. It uses such images, yes, but is capable of forming another kind which we see without the aid of the screen. We experience something similar with smell. It is possible to notice a distinctive perfume and then forget about it. Days later, even though we cannot call up any representation, we may suddenly realize that we experienced the same perfume years before. And, further, be able to recall not only the perfume, without its being present as a smell, but the exact circumstances as well—and so with images.

We may experience an image without seeing it on a screen, or being conscious of it as a pure abstraction brought forward by an act of reflexion after the image itself has passed, which explains why some poetry which has no obvious imagery in the accepted sense is often more effective than poetry made up of representations. It penetrates beneath the screen on which these ordinary images are cast and touches the mind where it can see in a way that is not the way of the eye.

Poetry, therefore, is not simply representational imagery held together by description or abstract statement. For while it may be possible to break it up, by analysis, into these and other categories, the components thus spread on the table are not poetry nor very closely related to it. The elements may be the

79

same, but in poetry changed by logic of imagination into something new. The means may vary from age to age, poet to poet, but the effect is always basically the same. Henry James, in the preface to the 1909 edition of *The American*, speaks of:

> the effort of the artist to preserve for his subject that unity, and for his use of it (in other words for the interest he desires to excite) that effect of a *centre*, which most economise its value. Its value is most discussable when that economy has most operated; the content and the 'importance' of a work of art are in fine wholly dependent on its *being* one: outside of which all prate of its representative character, its meaning and its bearing, its morality, are an impudent thing. Strong in that character, which is the condition of its bearing witness at all, it is strong in every way.

Art, we may allow, serves purposes outside itself—or may do. And pure art, burning purely in the beholder, does not and cannot exist. But art must first of all be art, the basic cohesion of which is arrived at through logic of imagination. The phrase, I may be told, is too vague. This I grant, but it will serve, in conjunction with what we have said about imagery, to point in the right direction.

But having said all this, with the unity of the *Pisan Cantos* in mind, I must draw attention to weaknesses on account of which we cannot place them among the highest poetry. The first and most obvious is the disjointed surface. And then there is this difficulty. Although it is a separate poem quite unrelated as poetry to the preceding seventy cantos, it cannot be understood without our knowing the earlier sections, much of Pound's prose, and of course the books he has read. The words, 'Since Waterloo nothing, etc.' in canto 80, cannot be understood unless we know chapter XI of Brooks Adams's *Law of Civilization and Decay*, in particular the sentence: 'Probably Waterloo marked the opening of the new era, for after Waterloo the bankers met with no serious defeat.' The words, 'Leave the Duke, go for gold', which follow, depend on our knowing the

Two Nations, and the next quotation, ' "Will never be used at home " ', upon our having some knowledge of Lenin on capitalism and imperialism. The Pisan section in no sense draws together the threads of the preceding cantos. It does not make sense of the rest, or in any way justify them. But it cannot be understood apart from them because they provide many of the necessary notes. The passage in canto 74, from 'plowed in the sacred field' down to 'Yu the guider of waters', depends on our knowing canto 53 and Pound's version of the *Unwobbling Pivot.* Venus, described in canto 76 as 'powerful' and 'dread', is, we gather, the same as, or connected with, the 'destroyer of cities' of the first thirty cantos. Everything certainly points to this. But why usury the destroyer should be regarded as evil and Venus the destroyer good, I have not been able to discover. One point, however, is clear: Venus, who keeps cropping up in the first seventy cantos, continues to do so in the Pisan section. When, in canto 76, Anchises lays hold of her flanks of air, Pound is repeating canto 23, and, if we keep in mind his idea of the sculptor seeing the form in air, echoing 24 and 51 as well. If, for the first time in four hundred pages, we feel that some, at least, of the digging is worth while, the constant need of information, without which many passages convey nothing at all, is nevertheless a serious weakness which will be increasingly visible in the following detailed discussion, in which for sake of brevity we shall limit ourselves to:

(1) Pound's use of Confucius

(2) The reappearing eyes and ghostly figures, not unconnected with the sex-as-inspiration ideas of earlier cantos.

Pound first met with Confucius in London about 1911; first saw a Chinese text of the *Ta Hio* (or *Unwobbling Pivot,* as he was eventually to call it) when in 1913 he received from Mrs Fenollosa her husband's papers. Confucius became his Philosopher, and in the early 1920s he devoted an entire canto to him. He also published two versions in English: *Ta Hio* in April 1928 and *Digest of the Analects* in June 1937. But we may date his interest as it applies here from the second half of 1937. 'During august and the first half of september', he wrote in 'Mang Tsze:

The Ethics of Mencius', 'I isolated myself with the chinese text of the three books of Confucius, *Ta Hio*, *Analects* and the *Un-wavering Middle*, and that of Mencius, together with an enorm-ously learned crib but no dictionary.' One result of this new beginning was that he published three versions in Italian during the war and one in English in 1947; another result was some of the most beautiful poetry in the *Pisan Cantos*.

'And with one day's reading,' he says in canto 74, 'a man may have the key in his hands.' If we are to get the most out of the Pisan section we must take the hint and read Pound's versions of the *Unwobbling Pivot* and *Great Digest*, which are what he is here referring to. But we must also read his version of the *Analects*, and, we must be aware, at least, of Mencius.

All told there are in the Pisan section more than fifty quota-tions or fragments from Pound's Confucian books, a number of which call simultaneously on several different passages or even different works. For example, 'What you depart from is not the way' on the opening page of canto 74, derives from the *Unwobbling Pivot*, Part 1, I, 2 ('what you depart from is not the process') and Part 3, XXV, 1; but we need to have the whole of Part 1 in mind in order to get what he is saying. The 'way' or 'process' is for Pound the 'total process' of nature or the universe. And what holds it together is 'the tensile light, the Immaculata' of the *Pivot*, of which 'There is no end to its action':

> Light tensile immaculata
> the sun's cord unspotted
> (canto 74)

By association of ideas rather than any philosophical thread Pound then equates the Confucian light with Erigena's:

> 'sunt lumina' said the Oirishman to King Carolus,
> 'OMNIA,
> all things that are are lights' . . .

And this in turn is meant to link up with 'in coitu inluminatio' six pages later. We must take this, or leave it, according to taste. There is nothing else to go on. Whatever Pound's

Erigena may be saying—he is only very distantly related to the great philosopher of that name—we have no means of connecting him with Pound's Confucianism because they are both much too vague: part of the dream, in fact, not of philosophy.

The line, 'What you depart from is not the way', already mentioned, joins with 'rain also is of the process' and 'the wind also is of the process' on the same page of canto 74. And these then connect (for everything, or everything good, is gathered to the one pivot) with at least a dozen other passages in the Confucian books and Pisan section, as follows: the man who has reached the highest level of Confucian wisdom, 'the highest grade of this clarifying activity', is to all intents and purposes at one with the 'process'; he is 'companion to the brotherly earth' (*Pivot*, 3, XXVI, 5), to which Pound adds this explanation: 'offers the cup of mature wine to the earth'. Thus we have the fragment, 'offered the wine bowl' in canto 74, which may be said to connect up with numerous similar fragments and look forward to the 'what draws as thou drawest' passage on man's relationship with the earth, in canto 82. Another mention of the 'process', in 74, is followed by:

> employ men in proper season
> not when they are at harvest

from the *Analects*. The ruler or employer who lives according to the 'process' will, in other words, arrange his business so as not to interfere with work that depends upon the rhythm of the seasons. And so in these cantos Pound speaks of 'rain altars', 'corn cat', 'humanitas', and the 'full humanitas' of Wei, Chi and Pi-kan, all of which draw on the Confucian books. Once we have grasped the idea of the 'process' many other lines and passages fall into place. The man who 'seized the extremities and the opposites' (canto 74) and the one who knows 'what precedes and what follows' (77), belong to, or work with, the same 'process' which made possible the agreement between Shun and Wan, a thousand years apart—which item, unfortunately, is only half-told in 77. We need to look up the essay 'Mang Tzse: The Ethics of Mencius' to get the full meaning: 'When the aims of Shun and Wan were set together, though after a thousand years interval, they were as two halves of a tally stick.'

Sometimes, as in the case of 'semina motuum' ('the seeds of movement') in canto 80, we are at a loss to know whether he is calling on Confucius or simply indicating the passage of time. In the *Pivot*, the 'hidden seeds' move slowly, but with continuing motion penetrate 'the solid', and, penetrating the solid, come 'to shine forth on high'. In the *Digest*:

> One humane family can humanize a whole state; one courteous family can lift a whole state into courtesy: one grasping and perverse man can drive a nation to chaos. Such are the seeds of movement [*semina motuum*, the inner impulses of the tree]. That is what we mean by: one word will ruin the business, one man can bring the state to an orderly course.

It is only, therefore, by stretching somewhat the meaning and possible connexions of some of the fragments that we can relate them to the Confucian books. Other passages lean heavily on the Confucian connexion:

> the sage
> delighteth in water
> the humane man has amity with the hills
>
> as the grass grows by the weirs
> thought Uncle William . . .
> (canto 83)

The sage and the humane man are from the *Analects*:

> He said: the wise delight in water, the humane delight in the hills. The knowing are active; the humane, tranquil; the knowing get the pleasure, and the humane get long life.

Place this beside Yeats's 'Down by the Salley Gardens' and we see how 'Uncle William' comes into it:

> She bid me take life easy, as the grass grows on the weirs;
> But I was young and foolish and now am full of tears.

Possibly this is a borderline case where the beauty compensates for the trouble involved. And it may, because of an underlying poetic unity, communicate some at least of its meaning without our being aware. But the dangers are obvious and the room for misinterpretation too wide. A page or so later is a passage beginning 'this breath wholly covers the mountains' and ending 'as it stands in the Kung-Sun Chow,' in which the meaning does come through whether we know the Confucian books or not, although knowing them certainly makes it easier. Only when at the end he uses three Chinese signs to draw the passage together do we need reference books and prior knowledge. It is not enough, for example, to discover that the signs depend upon Mencius and mean something like 'don't assist nature, let things grow naturally'. To get the full flavour we must have heard the Mencian parable of the man who helped his wheat to grow, and hurried it along, by pulling it up.

I see no other way at this point of bringing home the full extent of Pound's dependence on Confucius than by a bare list, and this would be intolerable. The student who wants to know will make his own.

Meditating at Pisa on the beauties that remained in his mind, after the collapse of so much he had given his life to, Pound began to see that the things remembered were somehow present with him in the detention camp. They began to stand forth as real things. He was, I think, discovering, though obscurely and without knowing it, what has been defined as the power of the mind to become what it knows without upsetting the principle of identity. It caused him to write some of the most haunting but elusive lines in the whole work, in which, unfortunately, we find him leaving off before he has embodied fully his conceptions in verse.

'The suave eyes, quiet, not scornful' first appear on the opening page of canto 74, as part of the 'process'. Later, Cunizza da Romano appears, 'there in the corner'. Ghosts move about him, 'in the timeless air':

> they suddenly stand in my room here
> between me and the olive tree . . .

There is, he says in one place, no rancour in this world in-
habited by his shades. And: 'there came new subtlety of eyes
into my tent', 'nor any pair showed anger'. And he goes
on:

> Saw but the eyes and stance between the eyes,
> colour, diastasis,
>> careless or unaware it had not the
> whole tent's room.

On another occasion it is a Dryad who comes. 'Your eyes,' he
says, 'are like clouds.' 'Dryad' was Pound's name for Hilda
Doolittle; but whether she has any part in the Dryad here is
impossible to say. Another time the tent is invaded by the
wraith of his 'first friend', possibly the pianist Katherine
Heyman, 'who comes talking ceramics'. I say Katherine
Heyman for several reasons. First, the date 1904 occurs nearby,
and in volume two of Pound's two-volume edition of Beddoes,
her name is incribed in Pound's hand and dated 1904. In
addition, he speaks elsewhere of his first friend as a musician and
we know that he wrote poetry to Katherine Heyman, and some
of her concert publicity, in Venice in 1908. And finally, when he
quotes from Beddoes in canto 80, some thirty-five pages further
on, we notice that he draws upon passages marked in his own
edition, passages which he incorporated into an article on
Beddoes in the *Future* of September 1917. This may seem to be
forcing the matter too hard. But he does often work in this way
and many another insoluble problem in the *Cantos* yields to this
method. For while the working of his mind is often simple and
straightforward, the process of discovering it is tortuous because
he has not told us what he is talking about. And because he has
not told us, we cannot hope even to approach the meaning
until we have explored possibilities and eliminated the ineligible.

The shades, when they appear, are located in the crystalline
world described or mentioned on numerous occasions throughout the work. It is the 'inverse of water, clear over rock-bed'. It
is as if the poet were the rock-bed, looking out into the crystal.
Sometimes he is merely a witness:

sky's clear
night's sea
green of the mountain pool
shone from the unmasked eyes in half-mask's space.

At other times, he is taken into the vision:

> The eyes, this time my world,
> But pass and look *from* mine
> between my lids
> sea, sky, and pool
> alternate
> pool, sky, sea, . . .

He does not think that these shades are souls or individual
personalities, nor yet that they indicate '*atasal*', or union with
God. There is a clue, perhaps, to what he is thinking about, in
Cheever Dunning's 'Shadows', published in Pound's anthology
Profile (1932) and mentioned obliquely near the beginning of
canto 76. Whoever or whatever they are, it is a world alive in
these one hundred and twenty five pages, but, as I said, never
quite formulated.

Chief among the shades is Venus. She might almost be said
to preside over the *Pisan Cantos*. And when another woman
appears we are never quite sure whether she may not in fact be
Venus in disguise, or that Venus Immortal may not be shining
through her. Half-way through canto 74 she rises from the sea,
blown ashore by Zephyr. We know her, Pound says, from her
manner of walking. She appears again, for a moment, about ten
pages later: the same vision, but this time she is riding the
seawaves in a great shell. A few lines later Cunizza comes; just
the name, nothing else, but accompanied by another, who
throughout the section identifies herself as the moon ('Io son'
la luna'). Within a few lines he is remembering:

> as against the half-light of the window
> with the sea beyond making horizon
> le contre-jour the line of the cameo

profile 'to carve Achaia'
    a dream passing over the face in the half-light
    Venere . . .

I always think of this passage as commemorating scenes in Rapallo during the 1920s or 1930s, with two photographs particularly in mind. One accompanies an article on Vivaldi by the violinist Olga Rudge, in the *Delphian Quarterly* of January 1938. It is of Olga Rudge herself: a silhouette against the light of the window. The other, also of Miss Rudge, accompanies an article by Pound on money and music, in the *Delphian Quarterly* of January 1936. It is almost full-face, but strongly suggests a cameo. What is probably the first mention of Olga Rudge in Pound's writings is a notice of one of her London concerts in the *New Age* of 25 November 1920, published under the pseudonym William Atheling. It is possible that the scene by the window in canto 74 links up with 'Fa Han and I' in canto 23. The phrase, 'to carve Achaia' which echoes Pound's *Mauberley*, is no doubt meant to remind us of Pisanello's mastery of the medallic art. And enables us to take up the thread two pages later when again he echoes *Mauberley*—a related passage—with the words, 'cheek bone, by verbal manifestation'. The eyes of the woman, he says in this second passage, are those of Botticelli's 'Birth of Venus'; 'the child's face' is to be found in a fresco at the Palazzo Capoquadri in Siena. The child, judging by canto 83 ('Maria's face there in the fresco'), is Pound's daughter Mary. And there is a reference to 'my little girl' ('mia pargoletta') in canto 80, as well as a conversation toward the end of 84, in which the by now grown-up daughter, visiting her father at the Pisan camp, discusses with him through the barbed wire the respective merits of the German and American armies in Northern Italy. Her home was at Gais, a village in the German-speaking Italian Tyrol. 'Tatile ist gekommen' in canto 78 is the child's 'Daddy has come!'

But returning to canto 74 and the 'child's face' in the fresco, the lines which follow continue his meditation on things held in the mind. First there is Venus, this time on a beach, under

Helios, the sun. The sun reminds him of 'the bright silk of the sunlight' in the *Pivot*, so he quotes from his Italian version, 'funge la purezza', meaning 'the tensile light, the immaculata' which functions without end. And this functioning of the 'process' is what causes these images to form in the mind and remain there in the place prepared for them. But not only to remain there, however, but resurgent; ever likely to issue in a new embodiment, as the art of Achaia in the medallions of Pisanello.

But this is only the beginning. Venus continues to appear throughout, also the women Pound associates with her: Cunizza, 'la luna', Botticelli's 'Primavera', Dirce, Ixotta, Dryads and Hamadryads. Also she who said, 'I still have the mould', in the sense of Dryden's lines to the Duchess of Ormond on her being cured of a sickness:

> And for that end, preserv'd the precious Mould,
> Which all the future Ormonds was to hold.

I have read, I cannot now recall where, that Pound's line refers to a woman who, when her son was shot by soldiers or partisans, retaliated: 'I still have the mould.'

These cantos, we must take pains to remember, are made largely out of association of ideas. Sometimes the association rises to metaphor; but more often that would be too strong a word. There is a good example in canto 80. A certain Sauter is there described as being unable to see the point of Whistler's portrait of Sarasate. Until, one day after Whistler's death, one identified simply as Ysaÿe, exclaimed on seeing it for the first time, 'What a fiddle!' Because of Sauter's dubious attitude we are at first inclined to read this remark as a jeer, despite a possible minor indication to the contrary. But the line which follows ('It is said also that Homer was a medic') sets us off on another track. We remember that Pound somewhere else has described Homer's anatomical accuracy as the ground upon which some commentator deduced him a surgeon. This Pound offered as an example of precision. And we remember then his hammering upon Pisanello's accuracy in painting horses.

Returning to Whistler we look more carefully at Sauter, Sarasate and Ysaÿe. The first apparently was a painter. Sarsate we recall was a musician. And Ysaÿe, according to the *Annotated Index*, was a violinist. And so the difficulty is solved. Sauter the painter was at first doubtful about the portrait, which he described as 'like a black fly hanging stuck to that canvas'. But when Ysaÿe came along, a violinist who knew violins, he recognized immediately in the painting a first-class fiddle. With the result, presumably, that Sauter was converted. On other occasions Pound adheres so strictly to the idea of concentration and elimination that he deletes the substance entirely. In this connexion it is not, perhaps, irrelevant to mention that an original typescript of the *Pisan Cantos*, by the author, with corrections in his own hand, which is in the possession of his daughter, contains essential phrases omitted from the published versions.

I am satisfied not to continue the practice of listing 'repeats' and echoes. Readers truly interested in this aspect will now be doing so for themselves. I have shown sufficiently already that in this respect the pattern of earlier cantos is continued here, which is all that is needed at this late stage of our enquiry.

VII

ROCK-DRILL 1955

THE *Pisan Cantos* constitute a separate poem, towards which the earlier cantos stand almost in the relation of notes or gloss. The reader who accepts this and our claim that it represents a return by the poet to his natural gift, will have no difficulty in accepting this further point that it is completely unrelated to *Rock-Drill* or *Thrones*.

From 1945 to 1958 Pound was in St Elizabeths Hospital, Washington, D.C. Both *Rock-Drill* and *Thrones* were composed there, although *Thrones* may have been added to or revised after his release in April 1958. Indications are, however, that the book was more or less in its present form before he left the hospital and returned to Italy. In St Elizabeths Pound was the victim of unusual circumstances. As soon as the young and not-so-young began to write to him from all corners of the world, as to a martyr, he took up again where he had left off in 1944. I will not dwell on the rubbish which we, his correspondents, fed to him, or the rubbish which he in turn fed to us. Some correspondents, I have no doubt, did better than this. But a good number of us, because we believed in him and (not least) sought his praise, helped to confirm him in the belief that he alone possessed a coherent view of the truth. It was his duty, therefore to hold out against The Enemy. I remember him speaking in all seriousness of the *Cantos* as a 'political weapon'. The Enemy understood this, hence the efforts to silence him —and a great deal more along the same lines. This may help to show why, after the humanity and breadth of much of the

Pisan section, the twenty-four cantos that follow are so false, pandering, as they do, to the poet's self-esteem. No longer is he following his bent, but proving himself right. Human perhaps, but not in itself enough to produce poetry.

In *Rock-Drill*, more perhaps than anywhere else in the *Cantos*, we are aware of the isolation, the separateness from the rest of the lyric fragments. 'Not led of lusting, not of contriving', he writes in canto 85, 'but is as the grass and tree.' This is basically the Pound of *A Lume Spento* and the early London years. And when, in canto 90, he writes of Hell ('out of Erebus, the deep-lying'), he is really only carrying forward a little what already he knew in 1912. It is not so much the beauty of the lyric moments that strikes us, as their fragmentary nature. Nor is there any place for them here, amid the manias ranged in tiers. But neither does the arrangement constitute a world. For if it is a world it is neither clear and formal enough to be understood and criticized, as, say, the *City of God*, nor yet sufficiently infused with tone and other necessary qualities to be judged as poetry. That these cantos can at times hypnotize I admit. But that is only one aspect of art, and *Rock-Drill* and *Thrones* know no other. In reading them again I am reminded of a correspondent who in 1938 wrote to Pound, 'What do you mean by *Ta Hio*? Is it a tax on money? If so, I think it need only be adopted in an emergency.'

At Giessen in 1911 Ford Madox Hueffer helped to purge the young Pound of artificial diction and set him on the road to a more natural language. But this was no safeguard against poor method. So that an error already, in 1911, being pointed to by von Harnack in Giessen, oddly enough, was committed by Pound many years later in his handling of occult and anthropological themes in *Rock-Drill* and *Thrones*. In *Wissenchaft und Leben* (II), von Harnack spoke of:

> this comparative mythology which endeavours to connect everything causally with everything else, which tears down solid fences, playfully bridges separating chasms and spins combinations out of superficial similarities. In this way [he continues], it is possible in the twinkling of an eye to turn

Christ into a sun god and the twelve Apostles into the twelve months of the calendar, to recall, when thinking of the nativity all the other stories of divine births, to let the dove of Jesus' baptism set us chasing all the other doves of mythology, to join all the other famous asses to the ass on which Jesus entered Jerusalem and so with the magic wand of 'comparative religion' to eliminate every original and spontaneous feature that a story may contain.[1]

It is no longer persuasive to link sun gods in Egypt with those in South America merely on the ground that they are sun gods. Discipline demands that we discover first what the Egyptians meant by theirs, what the tribes of South America by theirs, and understand them locally before hitching them together into a piece of comparative anthropology. The refinements of any subject are just as much in telling things apart which look the same, as in finding similarities in things which are different.

One of our objections to Pound in the later cantos is his inability to make poetic use of what he takes from others. A poem, if it is genuine, contains its meaning within itself. Not absolutely, so that it is an isolated entity, but sufficiently to have a voice of its own. The imaginative centre must be in the poem and not outside it. But that is not all: equally important is the poem's relation to tradition and usage. For the poetry grows in intensity as it approaches a traditional centre of meaning without actually touching it. Too distant from a centre, it tends to the inane. So close that it touches, to dullness and inertia. Tension comes of establishing originality within the field of attraction exerted by tradition, but still, as it were, separate from it, so that the originality is not overwhelmed. In this way, the traditional force of a word, without which a literature can scarcely exist, is turned to new creation.

And so the most effective originality is sometimes achieved by the smallest possible alteration to what has gone before. By fine variations within an accepted form or on an accepted theme,

[1] Quoted by Hugo Rahner, *Greek Myths and Christian Mystery*, London, 1963.

or by the extension of a form invented by earlier poets who did not, or could not, see the possibilities.

> A love that ebbs and flows, now up, now down;
> A morning's favour and an evening's frown.

This was written about 1599 and published in 1600. But it was not until Pope and Johnson that this type of couplet was brought to perfection. Originality in this sense is the ability to make new use of what has gone before. And what has gone before includes the ideas, rhythms and images of other writers. 'Still Dunce the second reigns like Dunce the first', says Pope, following Dryden's 'And Tom the Second reigns like Tom the First'. Goldsmith in the *Deserted Village* draws several times on Dryden's 'Lines to My Honour'd Kinsman', without loss to either. The only test, really, is success. There are few poets in English more original than Fitzgerald, who yet, one way or another, borrowed almost all he possessed.

DRYDEN:

> One woful day sweeps children, friends and wife,
> And all the brittle blessings of my life!
> Add one thing more, and all thou say'st is true;
> Thy want and wish of them is vanish'd too . . .

FITZGERALD:

> Oh, come with old Khayyam, and leave the wise
> To talk; one thing is certain, that life flies;
>   One thing is certain and the rest is lies;
> The flower that once has blown for ever dies.

It was Dryden who created the speech in which the *Rubaiyat* is delivered, but that speech is directed by Fitzgerald to ends of his own:

DRYDEN:

> When healths go round, and kindly brimmers flow,
> 'Till the fresh garlands on their foreheads glow,
> They whine, and cry, let us make haste to live,
> Short are the joys that humane life can give.

Rock-Drill 1955

FITZGERALD:

Dreaming when Dawn's Left Hand was in the sky
I heard a Voice within the Tavern cry,
    'Awake, my little ones, and fill the Cup
Before Life's Liquor in its Cup be dry.'

Ah, fill the Cup:—what boots it to repeat
How Time is slipping underneath our Feet:
    Unborn TO-MORROW, and dead YESTERDAY,
Why fret about them if TO-DAY be sweet!

Whatever Dryden provided towards the *Rubaiyat* he does not have any part in the final product. It is present, but no longer his; Fitzgerald has assimilated it. Now it is this assimilation which is absent from *Rock-Drill*, because while supposedly writing a poem, Pound is also trying to compile an anthology in which the quotations retain something like their original identity and meaning, and at the same time to annotate and use them for his own historical, religious and anthropological purposes. The first canto, to begin with, contains a hundred or more Chinese signs, the purpose of which, if it is not to impress, escapes us. This would be bearable if the English text were sharp and coherent, but it is not. We have cheap language masquerading as precision, as when he admonishes us 'Not to pamper this squirrel-headedness' and not to 'sit down on a job that is done'. And much of it is inert: 'We flop if we cannot maintain the awareness.' But even banality might be allowed if there were something else to make up for it. But just as we seem about to be rewarded for our patience, as with Windeler's vision in canto 87, he pulls up short and leaves it to the reader to discover that the rest of the story is in the postscript to his English version of Remy de Gourmont's *Natural Philosophy of Love*.

The work is not, for the reader who has had the time and patience to delve, the jumble it must appear to one who approaches it unprepared. The fragments often have a meaning, if we know about them or where they come from. And they do

often fit together, if one is willing to grant Pound's interpretation or viewpoint. Our objection is that the result is so often
neither poetry nor interesting. Canto 91 is a more extended
version of chapters 4 and 39 of *Kulchur*, but the latter is not
inferior and much easier reading. I once took the trouble to
trace, in the hope of making sense out of it, the ancient Egyptian
material in cantos 91, 93 and 94. With, I think, two exceptions,
the extracts are from two little books by the poet's son-in-law,
Boris de Rachewiltz: *Il Papiro Magico Vaticano* (Rome, 1954)
and *Massime degli Antichi Egiziani* (Milan, 1954). A third book-
let, *Liriche Amorose degli Antichi Egiziani* (Milan, 1954), is referred to in canto 95. I discovered that the princess Ra-Set
(91) is not actually a goddess or ruler, but created by Pound
from *Ra* the Egyptian sun god who is good, and *Set* who is evil.
The idea perhaps is that Set's evil is resolved in Ra's greater
goodness. I discovered also that the hieroglyphics at the start of
93 mean 'A man's paradise is his good nature', and that 'panis
angelicus' is inserted beside the name Antef because Antef is
recorded as having said 'I am food for the hungry and help for
the outcast'. I found out who Antef and Khati were, and
roughly when they lived, on what steles and papyri their words
are recorded, and in which museums the steles and papyri now
are. When Pound says, 'To Isis this incense' (93), he refers, I
was told, to the ancient Egyptian idea of incense as a medium
for transforming the material into the spiritual. I was able to
connect this and other information with a painting of, I think it
is 'Isis-Luna', by Sherri Martinelli, who used to visit Pound in
St Elizabeths and figures prominently, I have been told, in
Rock-Drill. A little book of reproductions of some of her work,
to which Pound contributed an introduction, was published
under the title *La Martinelli* in Milan in 1956.

With this knowledge in hand we are able to connect, for
instance, Antef, Augustine and the idea of abundance, on the
opening page of 93, with Alessandro, Saladin, Galasso and
Dante, four pages later. And connect these, in turn, with architecture. For the loss or giving up of the idea of abundance, and
decline in religion from Augustine's time to Michelangelo's

run parallel with the decline in architecture from San Domenico to St Peters. And the 'internal horrors' of St Peters reflect the vice of pastors who care for their 'flock' only for what they can get out of it. Not that Pound says it in quite this way. For canto 93, as indeed most of *Rock-Drill* and *Thrones* and many earlier cantos, is couched in a language which says everything and means nothing. Much of the time Pound has not thought out the connexions he makes, and does not therefore know what he is saying. But all too often, when we do trace through to a definite meaning, it proves not to have been worth while. In short, the material has not been assimilated; or, where it has, is seldom interesting, unless we happen to share, or for some reason wish to support, Pound's view of his subjects.

Cantos 85 and 86 are about government. That much, I think, is clear, even if we have reservations about the author's statement that 85 'is a somewhat detailed confirmation of Kung's view that the basic principles of government are found in the Shu, the History Classic'. Canto 86 is a brief history of Europe, or a collection of what Pound might call significant data on the history of Europe, from Talleyrand to Mussolini, with an occasional quick look at earlier periods as far back as Babylon. The idea, judging by the final page, is to prove that Pound was right and Roosevelt wrong. The quotation from W. E. Woodward is meant to show that the President was addicted to talking and giving advice, instead of listening and taking it from those who knew better. The reference to the 'Eleven literates' is meant to expose the poor quality of the United States Congress during the 1930s. It comes from a letter by Bronson Cutting, dated 9 December 1930. By 1939, as the final quotation indicates, the nation or its leadership was in hysteria, with the inevitable result: 'Bellum cano perenne', one more battle in the long war between 'the usurer and any man who wants to do a good job'.

Canto 87 continues the play of the same ideas, with the emphasis now on money. There is much less hope of keeping up with these cantos than the Pisan section, unless we come to them fully equipped. We will not know, for example, what 'perché si vuol mettere' stands for, unless we remember from Chapter 15 of *Kulchur* that it is part of Mussolini's question to Pound ('Why do you want to put your ideas in order?') when they met in 1932. The reply, 'for my poem' (meaning the *Cantos*), is given, not in 87, but in 93. The two fragments on the fourth page of canto 87, about 'Destutt or whomso', and metal as barter, are a complete puzzle unless we recall the fuller statement by 'Tracy' on the final page of canto 71. We happen to connect the two, because, no thanks to Pound, we discover that Tracy's full name was Comte Antoine Destutt de Tracy.

Cantos 88 and 89 contain here and there some of the poet's best writing, but only, I am afraid, if we have first read Thomas Hart Benton's two volume *Thirty Years' View: or A History of the Working of the American Government 1820 to 1850* (New York, 1854-56). Once we know the characters and the scene, the two cantos are seen to be an excellent reduction of certain points in the book, and a continuation, in an approximate sort of way, of canto 37. The Benton cantos may be said to reinforce the earlier, in so far as they tell of another part of the same struggle from a similar point of view.

The remaining six cantos are devoted to love and Eleusis. There are numerous political and economic interludes, either in praise of honour, virtue and justice, or as contrast with the Eleusinian paradise. But love, which is beyond civic order, is the main theme. It is love which has lifted him out of Erebus: 'You have stirred my mind out of dust.' The universe is alive to the initiate, who, permeated by, or transformed perhaps into, the spirit of Eleusis, finds entrance into the 'great crystal of paradise'.

The first of the six, canto 90, opens with a quotation in Latin from Richard of St Victor (d. 1173). In a letter dated 6 June 1954, from St Elizabeths, Pound told me that he had 'absorbed a lot' of Richard in 1908, but had not referred to him again until, it would appear, about the time of the letter. In his enthusiasm to communicate Richard's vitality and importance, he translated two passages: 'No contemplation without a certain vivacity of mind', and this, which is the one given in

Latin at the beginning of the canto: 'The human soul is not love, but love flows from it. It cannot have a good time in itself but only in the love pouring from it.' This and the canto illustrate one aspect of Pound's method of composition. Something strikes him as interesting. It is about love. Very well, he puts it in with other items about love, regardless of any subtler considerations. There is nothing in the wording, in the arrangement of the canto, or in the poetry to say how, if it is Richard's meaning we are concerned with, the love of the mystic can be reconciled with the rest of the canto. If the explanation is there, it is certainly not there poetically, which is what matters. Given certain information, we are able to say that canto 90 probably records a personal experience, of the man or the spirit ('to parched grass, now is rain'), which he places in the context of Eleusis—a tradition running, he implies, from the San Ku (an inner council in ancient China) to the Albigensians and the Templars, and including possibly Erigena. (By canto 105, incidentally, he is suggesting that 'They', meaning I suppose the orthodox, 'probably murdered Erigena', presumably for the secret knowledge he harboured.) When he invokes the dream in these cantos it is contrived, in the bad sense of the word. There is none of the naturalness and humanity of the *Pisan Cantos*.

The same experience of love is continued in 91, 92 and 93, where it is involved with continuously shifting aspects of the 'mysteries', as Pound calls them. One moment it is Danaë being visited by the god in Ecbatan, the next Leucothea aiding Ulysses, or 'Ra-Set in her barge'. What might be overlooked is that these three cantos, particularly 91, retell in tougher language, but much more confusedly, his ideas of 1906-11. I would point to, in particular, *Canzoni* and the poem 'Canzone: Of Angels':

> Three splendours, saw I, of high holiness,
> From clarity to clarity ascending . . .

The language of the cantos, we need hardly say, is better; and the mind that wrote them has seen more of the world. But the thought, basically, is the same. And when he takes in several new figures, such as Apollonius of Tyana, from the *Life* by Philostratus, the gain is purely quantitative. His knowledge has broadened, but not deepened. Nothing new has been felt, nothing new created. We have no sense of being on one of the frontiers of the human mind, or of new arrangement of words lighting up new-found territory; or even, for that matter, of the familiar seen through new eyes, from a different stand or under a different light; but only of further (superfluous, we might almost say) proof or illustration of something already dealt with. The lines from canto 92:

> 'And if I see her not
> no sight is worth the beauty of my thought.'

are not born of new perception. In feeling or knowledge they explore no new dimension, but belong, with the rest of the canto, to the Cavalcanti and Provençal studies of 1905-11. Reading the first line of his translation of 'Li Granz Desirs', published in Walter Morse Rummel's *Hesternae Rosae* (1913): 'The great desire sheds fragrance o'er my thinking', we may even wonder whether something has not been lost in the intervening years, or left unfinished. However this may be, we are distinctly aware, comparing works forty-five years apart, of a mind that has not matured. It is convenient and comforting to think always of style and mind as maturing together, in harmony. But here is a case where it is not so. As far as the *Pisan Cantos* are concerned, it could be shown that the moments —they are sporadic—of greater maturity are of an unusual character, imposed, one might say, from without, and gone again when the pressure lifted: not having become, that is, part of his mind, through habit, but the result of a meeting of exceptional circumstances with an exceptional man.

A passage in canto 93 is worth examining here for the example it affords of the difficulties we must be prepared to master in order to achieve even local understanding. Pound has been speaking of 'distributive justice', and what he calls 'agenda', or things that need doing immediately: 'All ov which,' he says, 'may be a little slow for the reader and seem platitudinous'. He then says, 'und kein Weekend-Spass' ('and no weekend-fun'), meaning we take it, that the reader who would understand what is going on in the world, must give full time to it. And then this:

> Mr Hoepli sent a small brochure to Svitzerland
> and his banker friend replied *'urgente'*:
> 'destroy it e farlo sparire.'
> Shivers has received (again) nomination
> and 'Alfalfa' is no longer in Who's Who,
> current issue.
> Grenfell's death was (like some others)
> suspiciously sudden.
> The Bard of Avon mentioned the subject,
> Dante mentioned the subject,
> and the lit profs discuss other passages
> in abuleia
> or in total unconsciousness
> Four thousand years after KATI . . .

Mr Hoepli belonged to the big Italian book distributors of that name. The 'small brochure' which he sent to Switzerland was Pound's *Lavoro ed Usura*, a reprint in 1954 of three of his wartime monetary pamphlets. The publisher of the reprint was Vanni Scheiwiller of Milan, whose father, Giovanni, was connected with the Hoepli organization. Mr Hoepli, so the story goes, sent a copy of *Lavoro ed Usura* to a banker friend in Switzerland. The banker, terrified or angered by the truth, sent an urgent telegram, or perhaps returned the book by express-delivery, at any rate warned Mr Hoepli to suppress it. The lines about Shivers and 'Alfalfa' are meant to illustrate another aspect of the same drive against the truth. But what aspect, exactly, is now hard to say. Certainly a full explanation would be impossible without having before us the various newsletters, cuttings and crank publications Pound was reading in 1953-54. I remember that Shivers was Governor of Texas and enjoyed a certain notoriety for a season or two, in the early or mid-1950s, but I cannot now be sure whether Pound was 'for' or 'against'.

Whether, that is, Shivers is to be counted among those who have fought usury or as one of its minions. 'Alfalfa', whose name was Murray, was Governor of Oklahoma about the same time. He is mentioned, not so much for anything that he himself did, I think, as for the fact that his father, an ex-Governor of the state, was author of a recent anti-Jewish book called *Adam and Cain*, published by the Meador Press of Boston. It may have been in this book that Pound first came across L. A. Waddell, some of whose works provide Sumerian and other motifs in cantos 94, 97 and elsewhere. At any rate, Murray, basing himself on Waddell, describes how the superior Aryan peoples have been undermined by Semites or other inferiors. The meaning in the canto is that because of this, or some related activity, 'Alfalfa' has been removed from *Who's Who*.

Grenfell, whose death, according to Pound, was 'suspiciously sudden', is supposed to light up yet another facet of the same 'war'. He was Captain Russell Grenfell, British naval historian and one-time head of the Royal Naval College. The book Pound had in mind was *Unconditional Hatred*, not published in England at the time, but only by the Devin-Adair Company of New York in 1954. Pound was much taken with it and drew from it several lines for canto 85, including 'Galileo index'd 1616' and 'Wellington's peace after Vaterloo'. As corrective to wartime nonsense about Germany being uniquely belligerent the book may have its points. But I am no longer sure that this is what Pound had in mind, only that he means us to gather that Grenfell was got rid of for his service to the truth. The subject mentioned by Shakespeare and Dante, and avoided by the 'lit profs', is of course usury.

Now it is not enough to know a little about these matters if we are to understand what Pound is talking about. We have to have read the books, pamphlets and cuttings, and to have heard the stories. Everything about the passage above, including the tone, depends upon our knowing the facts and having some definite appreciation of the atmosphere in which it was written. Until we actually look into the sources, handle the books, place ourselves in Pound's situation and see as nearly as possible through his eyes, we cannot even begin to know how the material is supposed to function. But function is too serious a word. It suggests the working out of a poetic design. Pound is not here composing poetry, he is keeping a kind of mental diary which includes snatches of poetry. And in this sense, and this sense alone, the matter and form are one.

VIII

THRONES 1959

WE ARE BETTER ABLE to follow what is going on in *Thrones* if
we know something about the eighty or more unsigned or
pseudonymous items which Pound contributed to the *New
Times*, Melbourne, from late 1955 until early 1957. They range
from a few lines each to more than a thousand words. Of
little or no interest in themselves they are nevertheless invalu-
able when it comes to understanding the working of the poet's
mind in this last section.

'The "poem" should,' Pound wrote in the *New Review* in
1931, 'theoretically, in its final stage of composition, swallow its
own notes'. The *Cantos* is not, unfortunately, such a poem. It is so
involved with its creator that we are unlikely most of the time
to have any idea what it is about unless we locate the precise
subject he was turning over in his mind at the time of composition. And while it is true that the *Cantos* is the diary of a
mind, it is of a mind moving: nomad, unsettled, that cannot sit
still and look at any subject for longer than it takes its highly
intelligent and quick-witted owner to frame in poetry a memo
or shorthand note, in prose a series of his often memorable
aphorisms. Pound is no visionary peering into the heart of things,
or the depths of the spirit. Of these he knows little, and this at
second hand. He is a brilliant collector of what he finds on the
surface of things. Even his choice of materials in the *Cantos* has
been governed very largely by the books which happened to be
beside him or within reach. We are dealing with a mind, which,
as it moves, takes this or that according to its need to see the

universe as consistent. But at the same time a mind which cannot wait to learn. Which means that when he wants to philosophize, for example, he ends up by giving us a list of names of philosophers.

In order to be able to follow, even roughly, canto 96, we must know first of all such direct sources as Paulus the Deacon and Nicole's edition of the Byzantine Eparch's edict. We must have also an idea of what else he was reading at the time, and, finally a good knowledge of what else he was writing. When he says that Brennus invited 'his wife to drink from her father's skull' it is possible that he has nothing more in mind than just that. It may be a colourful detail of no particular significance, as may be the case, I suspect, with one or two much earlier passages over which the critics have disagreed, while trying to read into them much more than is there. But a look at the *New Times* of 13 July 1956 suggests something quite different. There, under the initials M.L., Pound wrote: 'One should observe impartiality in ethnological studies, inspecting each living specimen as an individual but having provisional categories, and a table of symptoms, hammite or nordic—from our red-headed forbears drinking from the skulls of their enemies, to the kahal system....' When we remember that canto 96 was first published in the Spring 1956 issue of the *Hudson Review*, we are inclined, especially in view of evidence converging from other quarters, to the belief that Pound is here indulging in 'ethnological studies'. The line in canto 97, ' "Window dressing" as Bryan admitted to Kitson', is difficult unless we know the paragraph on William Jennings Bryan and the Free Silver Movement in Pound's *Introduction to the Economic Nature of the United States*,[1] and the following from his article 'An American Re-Examines Douglas', published in the *New Times* of 22 February 1957, under the signature George W. Gibson:

The silence surrounding Douglas's work from 1919 onward can be neatly accounted for, I think, by the open-

[1] First edition (in Italian), Venice 1944; first edition in English, London 1950; revised version in *Impact*, Chicago 1960.

ing of chapter VI (part 2) in *Social Credit*. And the Major's outline of the treatment accorded any attempt to break through the blackout of history has been illustrated by Ezra Pound's anecdote of Sir A. de P. Montagu Webb. As soon as this worthy admitted that he was running silver propaganda, in order to get the means of printing anything useful whatever; and that, of course, the real crux was credit, he was given a job in Karachi, much to his delight, as he did not recognise the move on the part of the enemy. William J. Bryan admitted to Arthur Kitson many years ago that the 'Free Silver' campaign was window dressing and that the real issue was the control of the nation's credit.

This does not perhaps enable us to understand the line any better, in the context of the canto, but does at least save us from thinking it means something else altogether. When talking of interest-rates in canto 99, and those who 'Dig up root to chase branches', he refers to 'Michelet & Ambrose "De Tobia" '. In Alexander Del Mar's *Middle Ages Revisited,* which Pound was reading at the time, is a quotation from Michelet's *History of Rome.* It may be this that he has in mind:

> As priests, the patricians exercised other vexations, over the people ... Under pretext of sacrifice, they took the finest ram, the best bull, from the plebian.

A clue to the 'Ambrose' may perhaps be buried in these lines, unsigned, but definitely by Pound, in the *New Times* of 13 July 1956:

> 'We accuse borrowers of acting imprudently', says St Ambrose in 'De Tobia', but there is nothing dirtier than the lenders of money (nihil nequius feneratioribus) ... They go after new heirs (aucupantur, they act as bird-catchers) and simulate paternal and avuncular friendship, wishing to know their domestic necessities. . pretend they themselves haven't the money. . .
>
> St Ambrose says that a fish swallows the hook without

seeing it, but you (the borrower) see it and swallow it. 'I
have seen sons sold,' he says, 'for their fathers' debts.'

What I have shown here with regard to the *New Times*
applies also, though not to the same extent, to such other
publications as *Strike* (Washington, D.C.), *Edge* (Melbourne),
Voice, Nine and *European* (England), *Mood* (St Louis), *Four Pages*
(Galveston, Texas), and perhaps even the *Idaho Lampliter*. When
Pound quotes from Burton Wheeler (canto 100), we cannot
really appreciate the precise standpoint unless we know the
unsigned lines, 'The Hour is Late', in the *New Times* of 29 June
1956 and the item headed 'Heritage', and signed N. B., in *Edge*
for March 1957, or similar items elsewhere. The mention on the
same page of the Louisiana Purchase depends on our knowing
something of Jefferson's original action and Pound's explanation of it in, if I remember rightly, *Voice*. Few I am sure would
understand the line on Danton (canto 100) without seeing the
context of Topino-Lebrun's statement on page 223 of the 1913
edition of Brooks Adams's *Theory of Social Revolutions*—if that
is what Pound is referring to. And fewer still, I suggest, would
be likely to catch the significance for Pound of the name Wiseman in the same canto. It was, I think, during his voyage to
America in 1939, or on the return trip the same year, that
Pound first heard it. He discovered soon afterwards that Wiseman, an Englishman and former head of British Intelligence in
the Western Hemisphere, was a member of the New York
banking firm of Kuhn, Loeb and Co. The name Wiseman
thereafter was synonymous with usurocracy. But whether, on
the other hand, this is an ingredient of the three lines in
question I cannot for certain say. I strongly suspect, for quite
independent reasons, that it is, despite the fact that the lines
refer to a period some ten years before Sir William Wiseman
actually joined the bank. But it is in the very nature of these
cantos to leave us the more uncertain the more we know about
them. The innocent reader cannot understand them, but takes
it for granted that time and patience will yield something. But
the more time we spend the more we wonder whether it is a

body of poetry at all. Until finally we reach a point where, taken as a whole, it looks like chaos. Such, I might add, as only a poet of Pound's skill and energy could have fashioned—but chaos, nevertheless.

Canto 96 is perhaps an attempt to register the stability of the Byzantine Empire and the reason for this, namely the guild system as it appears in the Eparch's edict. There are some good lines, but the overall effect is both monotonous and uncertain. Monotonous, because Pound goes on and on about Italian and Byzantine history without ever explaining what it is all about or what his point is. Uncertain, for a variety of reasons, but notably the laxness of mind and word, as when he says 'Mr Yeats called it Byzantium', ignorant of (hardly), or ignoring, the fact, that Yeats's Byzantium is far distant from his own. Both perhaps are imaginary, but it is slovenly to dump them together as if they were the same. Unless of course he is making a contrast, in which case why doesn't he say?

To make anything of canto 97 we must first have read Del Mar's *History of Monetary Systems* (Chicago, 1896), several chapters of which were published separately under Pound's guidance by the Square Dollar Press during the 1950s. But these booklets, *Roman and Moslem Moneys* and *History of Netherlands Monetary Systems*, do not contain everything that has found a way from the complete work into the canto. We have to know also the earlier cantos (' "I am sorry," said the London judge' refers back, for example, to canto 79), Pound's monetary essays, his *Indiscretions* (1923), and various items from his reading, including Yeats's statement, 'God has need of every individual soul'. But what, I wonder, are we supposed to make of the statement that 'in 1914 british sovereigns poured into the Philadelphia mint in great quantity and were promptly re-stamped with eagles'? Is he referring perhaps to the huge drain of gold to the United States during the First World War? If so then the restamping of sovereigns with the American eagle is, we take it, a sign of financial sovereignty passing from London to America. But we cannot be sure. And this uncertainty hangs over the whole canto. Sometimes a doubt is resolved by reference to Del Mar. Our question, who is Mons of Jute and why should he 'have his name in the record'? is answered on pages 278-9 of *Monetary Systems*:

It was not merely Norway and Sweden that rose up to throw off the shackles of Rome, it was all Scandinavia. Lubeck supplied troops and firearms, and the Chersonesus Cimbrica—that is to say, Jutland, or, as it is now called, the Duchy of Schleswick—transmitted to the tyrant of Denmark a demand of deposition which was read to him by a single unarmed man, the chief magistrate of the Jutes, whose act should never be permitted to fall into oblivion. This hero's name was Mons, and it deserves to be written over the gateway of every oppressor. The unlooked-for result of Mons' brave act was the abdication and flight of the cowardly Christian.

But when, soon after, we seek an answer to our question about Von Schultz and Sir William Harcourt—who they were and what exactly they did or said about 'national independence'— our pleasure in finding one is marred by discovery of a certain selectivity in Pound's adaptation. Von Schultz and Harcourt and what they said about a nation maintaining monetary independence, are indeed to be found on page 378 of Del Mar's *Systems*. But so also is Alexander Hamilton. Almost precisely the same thing as was said by Von Schultz and Harcourt, says Del Mar, 'was said by Alexander Hamilton a century previously'. But Pound, having already instructed his readers in canto 63 that Hamilton 'was the Prime snot in ALL American history', quietly removes him from Del Mar's list. The wording of 97, I might add, is sometimes excellent, but as poetry it has little to recommend it and is meaningless for long stretches even after we have consulted the sources.

Cantos 98 and 99 are taken largely from the *Sacred Edict* ('with a translation of the Colloquial Rendering by F. W. Baller, second edition, Shanghai, 1907—Prepared for Junior Members of the China Inland Mission'). Pound was excited by the *Edict* not only for the contents, which he greatly admired, but also for the effort made to take it down to the people by

having it put into the common language ('KOINE ENNOIA').
The '²muan ¹bpo' referred to in canto 98, has to do with
a ceremony performed in China, near Tibet, among the Na
Khi, who are mentioned again in cantos 101 and 104. Pound's
main source was a report by the botanist Joseph Rock, 'The
Muan Bpö Ceremony' in *Monumenta Serica*, Journal of Oriental
Studies, Catholic University of Pekin, Vol. XIII, 1948.[1]

There are signs here and there in these cantos of poetry: 'Rats'
gnaws, and bird's pecks: litigations'; but they are signs only.
They are nowhere worked out, and never sustained. And he
keeps falling back, as is now his habit, into slapdash: 'Get rid
of flimsy foundations', 'Cut the cackle', 'Plotinus his bellyache'.

Cantos 100-106 exhibit no special character or theme, either
individually or in combination. Scattered through them are a
number of items which for their understanding require 'inside
knowledge'. An example is the outburst, 'Oh GAWD!!! that
tenth section' in canto 100. It is supposed to register Pound's
consternation on discovering that the tenth section of the
American Constitution is an effective barrier to certain
monetary reform proposals. But that is not all. It carries, or
rather, was meant to carry, an additional meaning which anyone not in touch with Pound at the time of his discovery is
unlikely to be in a position to appreciate. We have to think,
first, of the poet in St Elizabeths, building up by personal contact and correspondence a following consisting largely of young
people interested, some more, some less, in monetary reform.
The basis of reform in America was to be the Constitution,
which he never ceased to praise as adequate for all such
purposes if only Americans would return to it and honour it as
the Founders intended. He was momentarily thrown off
balance when, after some ten years of this, he discovered that
the tenth section rules out what, in canto 96, he calls 'local
control of local purchasing power'. The line as it stands, in
canto 100, communicates none of the background essential for
its understanding.

[1] A traveller who has been there tells me that *Muan Bpö* or *²muan ¹bpo* is
pronounced something like *mwon purr*, but without sounding the *r*'s.

In canto 101 we are informed out of the blue, 'Del Pelo Pardi came on cunicoli'. Nothing more until canto 103 and the words 'cunicoli, canalesque'. No amount of goodwill on the reader's part can here make up for the absence of elementary communication. Del Pelo Pardi was an Italian interested in the history and pre-history of agriculture. His name and a little about him were known to some of Pound's associates and correspondents during the 1950s. Some, I think, had seen a little book or article which Pound was having translated into English. But it was not until I enquired of the poet's son-in-law, Boris de Rachewiltz, who had worked with Pelo Pardi, that I was able to see what Pound apparently meant. It seems that Pelo Pardi discovered not far from Rome ancient canals ('cunicoli') which he identified as a perfectly engineered irrigation system. But judging by the geological evidence they were far too old by many thousands of years to fit in with established chronology. But even this doesn't settle for us Pound's interest. It is not until canto 116, published in the *Paris Review* (Summer–Fall, 1962) that the word 'cunicoli' appears next to the statement, 'a little light in great darkness'. Del Pelo Pardi, we gather, is being honoured for his contribution to history and for daring to fight the 'historical blackout'. Here are a few more examples of his failure to communicate:

'*The libraries*' (*Ingrid*) '*have no Domvile.*' *Jan 1955* (canto 102) refers to the fact that Pound received from a correspondent in London a letter saying that she could not find anything by Sir Barry Domvile in local libraries. But even this means nothing unless we know that Pound was thinking specifically of Domvile's autobiography *From Admiral to Cabin Boy*, a comparatively mild piece of anti-semitism published in 1947 by the Britons Publishing Society. A poem by Domvile, 'Home-Thoughts from an Old Lag', is published in the appendix to Pound's *Pavannes and Divagations*, 1958.

Old Rocke (*with an -e terminal not the botanist*) *learned Abyssinia* (canto 104): Colonel Rocke was an Englishman active on behalf of Italy during the Abyssinian war, who disseminated information that was being refused circulation in Britain and elsewhere. He is not to be confused, Pound is saying, with Rock the botanist who wrote about the Muan Bpö.

'*Dalleyrand Berigorrr!*' (canto 105): According to Pound in conversation, 1960, a wealthy Jew, David Blumenthal, bought what had been successively Bertran de Born's and Talleyrand's home at Perigord, in Southern France. One evening at dinner a guest asked what the initials D. B. on the cutlery stood for. Blumenthal replied: 'Dalleyrand Berigorrr.' Pound meant it perhaps to be admired as an example of Jewish quickness and wit, but there is a shadow also of the Jew taking over what by skill and tradition the Gentile had built up over eight hundred years.

The reader will have noticed that on a number of occasions as far back as canto 86 Pound has mentioned 'Eva'. It was 'Eva's pa', he says, who heard the telephone conversation between the German Ambassador, von Hoesch, and Edward VIII, which, as we learn if we follow the fragments through *Rock-Drill* and *Thrones*, kept the peace for three years and was the reason 'they had to get rid of him', meaning the Duke of Windsor. Finally, on the penultimate page of canto 109, Pound quotes 'Monro', who was the Rome correspondent of the London *Morning Post*, as saying that Windsor would have to be got rid of because he might refuse to sign mobilization papers for war. The 'Eva' of this story is Eva Hesse, Pound's German translator, whose father was a diplomat with the German Embassy in London. In canto 102, Miss Hesse is praised for having improved, in her translation of the *Pisan Cantos*, the line, 'free speech without free radio speech is as zero.'

Of the authors we need to know, I will limit myself to three, mainly in order to illustrate my contention that the poem has by now deteriorated into a game for initiates. First, Alexander Del Mar. In canto 100 we find the word 'monetary (218 a.d.) commission' squeezed in between 'Shingled flakes on a moth's wing' and Belisarius forbidding his cavalry to ride through grainfields. The only monetary commission which seems to fit the case is this on p. 23 of Del Mar's *Ancient Britain Revisited* (New York, 1900), although the date there given is B.C. not A.D.:

There was a banking class in Rome, but it was probably absorbed by the Pontificate before Britain was permanently settled. A governmental Monetary Commission, consisting of three bankers, was formed so early as B.C. 218.

Later in the same canto Pound writes 'Half the land, and slaves or how much belonged to the temples'. The immediate source is *Ancient Britain Revisited*, p. 60:

As the established (pagan) church owned half the lands and slaves of Europe, avidity may have also had something to do with it.

But we must read also pages 105-10 of Del Mar's *The Middle Ages Revisited* (New York, 1900). To find out 'what happened' in the lines, 'And as for what happened after the king lost exclusivity even Del Mar gasps with astonishment' (canto 104), we must turn to chapter XIII, 'The Netherlands', in Del Mar's *History of Monetary Systems*:

Is it yet clearly understood that whatever degradation of money was committed by the emperors, whatever debasement was afterwards committed by the kings, these have since been vastly exceeded by the dishonest use made of 'individual' coinage and control of bank issues?

And more in the same chapter.

The second author we must know is L. A. Waddell. When Pound says (104):

> Once gold was
>   by ants
>   out of burrows

we are completely at sea unless we know this from page 13 of Waddell's *Indo-Sumerian Seals Deciphered* (London, 1925):

The gold-digging 'ants' are described by Strabo as having 'skins as large as leopards'. They were evidently the large Tibetan rabbit-like marmots, which burrowed in the auriferous sand and brought gold to the surface. On my visit to the source of the Sutlej at the Manasarowar Lake at

Mt Kailas in Tibet in 1900, I observed how numerous were
the marmots and their burrows on the plateau, some of the
animals standing nearly two feet high.

It might be argued that the meaning is clear enough in the context of the poem without our having to know the exact source;
that the idea of ants bringing gold out of burrows is a contrast
which illuminates the foolishness of man in digging it out as
treasure. But this would be unacceptable, and for this reason.
The lines and their surroundings are so eccentric it is impossible
for us to focus in this way. With nothing to guide us, we cannot
begin to work out what the lines mean in the poem until we
have found out what they mean by themselves. Which means
consulting the Waddell. And even if we discover that the source
is no part of the canto, the search has been necessary. For the
passage is so peculiar, so lacking in definition, any meaning
might be the right one. We have had to return to the source in
order to eliminate it. And this applies to almost every page of
Rock-Drill and *Thrones*.

The third author, Kuan Chung, Pound first read in May or
June 1957, when a Chinese poet living in the United States
sent him an extract from *Economic Dialogues in Ancient China*,
Selections from the *Kuan-tzu*, edited by Lewis Maverick and
published at Carbondale, Illinois, in 1954. Pound sent the
extract to me for publication in the magazine *Edge*, where it
appeared immediately, in the issue of June 1957. In canto 106,
which must have been written soon afterwards, he refers on the
first page to 'NINE decrees, 8th essay, the Kuan', which might
be heavy-going even for a Sinologist, unless he was able to
recall off-hand that what Pound calls 'the Kuan' is the *Kuan-tzu*,
and that Essay VIII, on the 'Basic Methods of Government',
includes:

At the 8th assembly, this regulation: '(Any Prince) who
establishes the four principles and puts them into practice
is to be commended to the minister of rites, as deserving a
grant of honour from the Three Lords (at the Emperor's
Court).'

114

Which in Maverick's edition is supported by this footnote:

> The four principles are: (1) do not dam up irrigation streams, depriving neighbouring states of water; (2) do not prohibit the export of food to neighbouring states; (3) do not displace rightful heirs of another state; (4) do not elevate a concubine to the position of wife.

On the second page of the same canto, the line 'all goods light against coin-skill' depends on our knowing the chapters in Maverick's book devoted to government control of monetary policy. We know better what Pound is talking about in cantos 107-109 if we consult Coke's *Institutes* and Catherine Drinker Bowen's life of Coke, *The Lion and the Throne*. Pound describes Coke as 'the clearest mind ever in England' (107) and it is the *Institutes*, I think, rather than Magna Carta itself, which he refers to as 'our PIVOT', meaning the English equivalent of Confucius' *Unwobbling Pivot*.

The system of unresolved implications out of which the *Cantos* are composed was in the earlier stages largely a matter of accident. I do not think that Pound was conscious of the effect it would have on the reader or of where it would lead. If later, as I suspect, he became aware to a certain extent of the ambiguous nature of the work, there was little he could do—unless he chose to abandon it, or rethink it entirely—except acquiesce in the consequences: in a mixture, that is, of the not quite poetry with the not quite history, which pretends to be both, the history raised by its association with the former into a higher knowledge. He continues in the same manner in the cantos which have appeared since the publication of *Thrones* in 1959. When, in canto 116, first published in the *Paris Review* in 1962, he speaks of his 'many errors', we cannot in all conscience welcome this as a genuine 'change of heart'. Offered outside the work it would be acceptable even without proof that the author knew what his errors were. But stated thus *in* the *Cantos*, in the same commanding manner as *Rock-Drill* and *Thrones*, it implies not only that he understands where he went wrong but that this discovery and admission have somehow been incorporated into the fabric of a long and coherent work now nearing completion.

In canto 114, first published in the October 1965 issue of the German magazine *Text+Kritik*, he writes: 'nor began nor ends anything'. This again, I claim, is indefensible. Apart from the difficulty in relating it to the Confucianism of the Pisan section (the 'things have ends and beginnings' of canto 76), we are being asked to accept that Pound is still master of the situation. Nature, history and culture, he implies, have been caught by the poet and channelled through a work, which is so constructed without beginning and without end, that it can encompass anything and everything.

We noted from the start Pound's inability in the *Cantos* to write sustained passages, or to join the passages together, musically or any other way, into larger units, and thence into cantos, each one self-contained yet part of the whole. I would draw attention to, in this regard, the endings to cantos. The desperate flourish, in almost every case, with which Pound tries to make it appear that some definite performance, having gone its measured course, is now being concluded, or has prepared the way for something to come. This does not apply in any general way to the poetry up to and including *Lustra*, most of which comprises short poems firmly controlled from beginning to end. But *Propertius*, his first attempt at a major poem, while it is important, betrays just this weakness we have noticed in the *Cantos*. It is not really a poem, but pieces of poetry. *Mauberley* is an exception; but not quite. Much of the perplexity it has given rise to is from ambiguity of form and intention no less than of surface. The ironic pose, the aloofness, refusal to explain, sudden cuts and juxtapositions, all serve the same purpose as in the *Cantos* the rather too-smart endings. He does not write poems, but poetry. And if sometimes the importance to him of what he is doing in the *Cantos* (forging 'a weapon'), and the desire to get it done and to show that the universe is a coherent whole, generate a field of force which holds the parts together, we ought to see this for what it is. It is not form, only the urge towards form, or at most the primitive beginnings of it. The *Cantos*, as a result, do not constitute a poem, but a disjointed series of short poems, passages, lines and fragments, often of exceptional beauty or interest, but uninformed, poetically or otherwise, by larger purpose.

INDEX

Index

Index